PEACE
IN THE
PARISH

PEACE
IN THE
PARISH

How to Use
Conflict Redemption

Principles and Process

JAMES QUALBEN

LANGMARC PUBLISHING • TEXAS

Cover design by Susan Q. Reue

LANGMARC Publishing
P.O. Box 33817
San Antonio, Texas 78265-3817

Printed in the United States of America
Library of Congress Cataloging in Publication Data

ISBN: 1-880292-00-9

To Loey

Contents

In Appreciation

Who among us can perform a complete opera by ourselves, especially when, like me, you never quite got the knack of playing a violin or sousaphone? My beloved wife and each of our children have performed this opera with me. For years, we have pressed on together through our Peace in the Parish project. Susan, Steven, and Michael and our son-in-law, David, love our Lord and the Body of Christ as much as Loey and I do. They have shared an overriding purpose that has pulled us through marshes of frustration and hardship enroute to making this book happen.

Because of heartfelt concern for the church's vitality, Drs. Paul and Ruth Qualben have given timely support and encouragement which made possible the design and writing of this book.

While so many congregations, pastors and lay leaders have provided the range of experience underlying *Peace in the Parish,* six colleagues in the Lutheran Church-Missouri Synod deserve thanks from those who will benefit from this enterprise. Ralph Bohlmann, LC-MS President, made the first moves which got a bold venture underway. Robert Sauer, then First Vice President, began as my "boss" but became my brother. From August Mennicke, current First Vice President, I learned first hand the "evangelical heart of Missouri." Norman Sincebaugh, District President, typifies his prayerful concern by his computer's daily opening password: "Qualben." Pastor Phil Esala has worked hand-in-hand with us from the beginning of all this. Arnold Kromphardt, retired District President, has been a warrior for Peace in the Parish.

Lisa K. Wilson's editorial expertise helped us refine the book's structure and style. Then, there was Roy Gilbertson who, while an ALC Bishop, talked me into this ten years ago. I have a hunch that heavenly hallways resound with laughter over Roy's Norwegian jokes the way his convention foyers did.

INTRODUCTION

P *eace in the Parish* is a hopeful book, especially for members and pastors who have known church conflict to be a disheartening mystery. This volume is addressed to clergy and lay people who care deeply for their church but are frustrated by its inability to work constructively with conflict.

The purpose of this book is to share with you the insights gained from my work on-site with nearly a hundred troubled congregations over the past eight years. No new approach has been more carefully verified within parish life.

There are five pastors in my immediate family including my deceased father, two brothers, one of our sons, and me. In the 1800s my wife's grandfather ventured in a covered wagon across North Dakota to serve a parish. Her uncle knew parish ministry's delights and hurts so well. Our family is entrenched in the church, and we love it deeply. We crave to see it restored to vitality, through the same compassionate love we know personally in Christ.

Growing up in a congregation that had its share of fights, I recall how they still got the job done. The Apostolic church had much more conflict than any present-day church, but out of their conflicts came renewal and outsurging mission. A congregation does not get into trouble because of conflict. It is conflicted because more important purposes no longer call the shots in day-to-day functions and choices. Conflict Redemption, then, is an *expectation* with a durable history backing it up. Its value is measured, not by tourniquets for stemming blood loss, but by vitality. No longer do we have to settle for such trivial objectives as resolving the issues, which never *are* the Issues anyway.

We are acutely aware that people would rather avoid conflict than deal with it or read a book about it. For years there have been well-intentioned attempts to import secular conflict resolution methods for church use. While we can learn something of value from such approaches, relying on them for church systems is like trying to hold the Olympics on Mars.

Conflict Redemption

You may be surprised to see the word *redemption* associated with conflict. Ordinary usage speaks of conflict *resolution* or *management*. *Peace in the Parish* describes a fresh approach to conflict based upon old and solid principles we have adapted for a thoroughly tested process. Conflict Redemption is a distinctive interaction of principles and processes which targets the "ecology" of church conflict.

This conflict ecology is *purposeful*. It is *belief-ful*. It is *systemic*. These are the three main principles of Conflict Redemption. They provide the system with its realism, dynamism and advanced simplicity.

- *Purposeful*. Conflict keeps most people from developing mutual purposes (or "so thats"), and lowers these purposes down to trivial levels such as win/lose or win-win strategies. All key components of Conflict Redemption work *so that* more important things will happen, including the rebuilding and invigoration of corporate Purpose Systems.

- *Belief-ful*. In Conflict Redemption, we are putting our beliefs to work purposefully! Purposeful reliance on the doctrine of Grace, for example, changes how we see each other and our relationship. Why? *So that* our agendas and expectations during times of strife are pulled to higher levels by doing unto each other as Christ has done unto us. Biblical doctrine gives vivid substance and clarity to the light shining at the end of what used to feel like a long, dark tunnel.

- *Systemic.* Church members have a habit of blaming lightning rods instead of storm systems for short-circuits and loss of power. "If only we can get rid of that lightning rod, our storms will go away." That naive avoidance gimmick reveals a mortal flaw in how too many of us view the church.

If you see your congregation as a bunch of fluttering leaves and twigs (individuals) without regard to the living vine-and-branches (the whole), you will neglect the possibility of your congregation's *systemic* vitality. A key to church systems' vitality is not "strong leadership," but a *shared* Purpose System. Conflict Redemption helps us "discern the Body" beyond members' tinkering, so that we can get on with knowing and growing in that Body of Christ.

Church conflict defies the usual tidy 20-step denominational cookie-cutter "program." Like history, church conflict is disorderly conduct. Therefore these pages provide many how-to's without regimenting how "it has to work" for everybody. I do my best to describe and explain such common ingredients, but their proportionate presence in any church's recipe is distinctive, requiring initiative and responsibility on your part to appropriate these insights for your situation.

The first five chapters are about congregational Purpose Systems, purposeful reliance on doctrine, and using the Five Steps of Matthew 18.

Chapters 6 through 14 draw heavily from my own experience working on-site (three to four days each) with those one hundred congregations. Occasions for Conflict Redemption and ways of moving from conflict to church vitality are explored.

Chapters 14 and 15 includes the text of some specific Usages and more How-To's we developed in working with congregations. I have summarized information on how to select, train and use the newly-adapted ancient precedent of Audicators.

There are no magic wands here. Where there is bad faith, or where members really have no confidence that Christianity *works*, the "success rate" for Conflict Redemption collapses for them. But for those who believe God's Word can work for them, Conflict Redemption's "success rate" is no less—nor more—than the Gospel's!

Except where I am describing actual on-site examples, references to clergy are gender-vague. Many examples refer to male pastors because thus far the majority of my consultations have been with LC-MS congregations. The other consultation congregations were served by male clergy.

I hope *Peace in the Parish* encourages and informs you as your church and ministry continue their journey toward new life and vitality in Christ. My wife Lois and I have been praying for that outcome throughout the years of discipleship which have led to these pages.

Cordially in Christ,

Jim Qualben

Terminology

Peace in the Parish began as a philosophy, developed as a nationwide project, and then designed its method. Because "conflict resolution" philosophies and methods have not worked well in churches, we set out with three basic objectives: (1) put doctrine to work; (2) focus on the corporate Body; and (3) seek redemptive outcomes. This meant going back to the drawing boards to locate solid foundations upon which an effective process could be constructed. To accomplish these objectives, the Lutheran-Church-Missouri Synod took on full support and oversight of the "Peace in the Parish project." Because I am not an LC-MS member, an unusual title was given my contracted role in project development and field-testing of resources: "National Consultant." With exceptional synod-wide support for the project, I worked in this full-time role for more than four years. I have traveled over 500,000 miles throughout the Missouri Synod working with congregations and Districts and institutions, with pastors, teachers and laity. Pulling together such experienced procedures and resources into a larger pattern is the basis for this volume. For several years now, the range of site consultations has extended to other church bodies.

Outsurge is used instead of "outreach" in this book partly because it associates with vitality more than with accumulation or grabbing. More to the point, I think it better expresses the biblical command to *go forth*. A church that is surging outward is not "getting new members" but winning souls for Christ. It is not enriching its organizational self-interest but Christ-Caring in that nearby world God so loved. An outsurging congregation does not feed on its members but plants seed for harvests in their Monday's world. "Outreach" reminds me of cult groupies confined in their airport booths calling to me with outreaching arms: Sir, Sir! Can I talk with you, Sir!

Christ-Care refers to an historic European heritage of mission-minded caregiving through the church's small groups. Technically, these small groups are PEG's (Purpose Embodiment Groups) rather than "felt needs" or affinity-based associations. The term first appeared in Luther's Nativity sermons at Wittenberg, first connected with small groups in 17th century Halle, paralleled by John Wesley's "Class," and most durably redefined by the mission movements in Norway (from the 1790's) and Neuendettelsau (from the 1840's). Because of their track record of sustained vitality within the larger church, *without* schism, along with the movements' simple procedures for assuring Christ-care's permeation throughout a congregation, we describe ways for their adaptation to American churches in Lois' *Christ-Care* Bible Study book and my *Church Vitality* book.

1

Purpose Systems

---◻︎---

"**S**o That" is one of the Bible's most frequently used phrases. With its corollaries, it also signals one of Scripture's basic themes: *purpose.* Christ comes to seek and save the lost *"so that* in Him we might have eternal life." Aha! But have you ever seen treatises or a basic seminary course offered on this? Have you heard of parents teaching "So thats" to their children? Children may have the impression that God's favorite word is *"Don't!"* since it resounds so frequently in our households. Virtually every major instance of God's redemptive action is revealed with explicit purposes, especially in the New Testament. God acts *purposefully!*

Does your congregation act purposefully, not only theoretically but in everyday reality as God does? Or, is it more a case of your church's operation reinforcing belief in Original Sin? We know all too well that congregations are driven by all sorts of corporate character defects. Recognizing this can have a blessed outcome: *so that* the Holy Spirit might lead us to redemption in Christ. Does it follow, then, that we should resolve to become more purposeful only in *spiritual* matters but leave *practical* matters to business as usual?

God does not do it that way. Episode after episode in Scripture, it was precisely in *practical* things where God's redemption came into people's lives by purposeful connection with their daily work. The woman at Jacob's well is just doing her job when she meets a man who turns out to be the long-awaited Messiah. So typical of God, almost a compulsion: to surprise us with the most stunning revelations of His presence and purposes while people are caught up in life's ordinary stuff. Can it be that same way at your church?

No "So Thats" in Your Kitchen

Members complained that three particular men never showed up for Work Days around church. "But they keep spending weekends at that Retreat Center scrubbing pots and pans in the kitchen. They even pay $65 each to do it!"

As is too typical for young mission-start churches, it was happening here. Three to five years after moving into its first building, Bethany's members were suffering from volunteer burnout. These three fellows had become one of its lightning rods.

"Why do you guys do it?" I asked about their menial work at that Center.

"So that first-timers can benefit from almost three more hours of special workshops which they could not get if they had to take turns on K.P. That is why we do it."

"So that...what?" I pressed.

"So that they can go back to their congregations and help get things moving."

"So that...what?"

"So that their churches can do better at helping people come to know Christ and follow Jesus."

I explained to the congregation "There are no *So Thats* in your kitchen. For this reason many of you are burning out, feeling more drain than gain in what you do here."

Getting into their building had taken a great deal of hard work and a lot of debt. There were many jobs to be done. It had seemed exciting at the time. Those were good purposes but not good enough to support higher levels of motivation. They were experiencing what almost amounts to a universal law: the lower our purposes, the lower our response.

Not all purposes are created equal; some are more important than others. Those higher purposes can influence, transform and interact with lesser purposes. In other words, there is such a thing as a *Purpose System:* distinct levels or ranks of purposes, interacting as a "system."

How specific and deliberate are the *so thats* at your church? You may have plenty of "good" low-level *so thats,* but if no higher *so thats* are actually calling the shots at church, expect low participation and response levels. This happens to congregations whose corporate purposes have collapsed.

There are markers of a collapsed Purpose System, a collapse which explains *why* churches either go conflict-dysfunctional or seem incapable of moving out of low gear. Before considering the markers, an explanation of Purpose Systems is in order. A robust corporate Purpose System is crucial for how well you cope with other obstacles on your way to church vitality.

Purpose System Defined

"Purpose System" refers to those interactive principles governing choices made by a person, a relationship, an organization or corporation. A Purpose System constitutes our shared sense of *Why*, including our goals and responsibilities. Purposes have to be ranked as to their relative importance, but not in a pyramid or hierarchy. That is why we have to emphasize their "interactive" nature. Otherwise, we end up with hierarchy's false choices, such as: which comes first, your career or our marriage?

Apostolic Purpose System

The *Apostolic Purpose System* model we use is the only one currently available which helps harmonize individual and corporate Purpose Systems. Adapted from the system which Paul and the apostolic church originated, there are four levels or dimensions of purposes. Paul radically changed the rabbinic "hierarchy of values" into an interactive *system* of purposes.

- **Personal Preference Purposes**
- **Organizational or Well-Being Purposes**
- **Identity Purposes**
- **Overriding Purposes**

Here are those four dimensions, beginning with the lowest (Level 4).

PERSONAL PREFERENCES
(Lowest—or fourth level—Purposes)

Personal Preference can be good and desirable, but it should have inferior importance. Examples of this lowest purpose level include: Lifestyle preferences, likes and dislikes, doing something nice for somebody because it makes both of you feel good. How important popularity and interpersonal skills are for you. Gauging how well your church is doing by how well people get along with each other. Voting with Harry on the building program because you owe him a favor. Pastors who gauge whether they are doing a good job by how much people *like* them.

ORGANIZATIONAL/WELL-BEING PURPOSES
(Better—third level—Purposes)

These purposes are less self-centered. Meeting the budget, administration and structure, doing things decently and in order lodge here. Balancing the checkbook, regardless of how spiritual you are. Buying that new home so that the family will be better off. This third level also is the purpose realm where control and power players thrive. None of the troubled congregations I have worked with were functioning higher than on this purpose level.

IDENTITY PURPOSES
(Staying power—second level—Purposes)

Identity purposes focus whatever identifies us within the larger scheme of things. As an example, for Lutherans doctrine and the authority of Scripture are on this higher level of importance. Episcopalians usually locate apostolic succession here, lowering doctrine and Scripture to the third level. The difference is between the integrity of our message being more important than just something "nice to have." However, *Identity* purposes must point to and exist for the sake of sustaining our *Overriding* purposes—as in Message for Mission! Otherwise, Identity purposes collapse down to the lower two purpose levels—as when orthodoxy becomes a political football.

OVERRIDING PURPOSES
(Highest—first level—Purposes)

Overriding Purposes are long-term and outsurging purposes which pull all other purpose-levels into alignment and energize them. However, to qualify for this unifying importance, an Overriding Purpose must be:
  —*participative:* any member must be able to own it through existing skills and experience;
  —*interactive:* must enable all purpose-levels to interact harmoniously;
  —*permeating:* it must permeate the congregation, throughout official and unofficial associations and functions;
  —*motivating:* the specific purpose has to provide motivational support for members' highest level of aspiration.

The word *interactive* keeps recurring because it is a good measure for a Purpose System's integrity. Where this interactive feature is lacking or ineffective, we often see the usual Mission Statement scenario: a shopping list of organizational fantasies which never actually call the shots.

There is a chain of restaurants I sometimes frequent on my travels. On a wall behind the cashier is this big brassy Mission Statement. But it has *never* influenced the caliber of service I have seen at these places. Is that what your church's Mission Statement amounts to?

Market-Message-Mission

The controversy over how market-driven a church should be can be clarified by reference to Purpose Systems. A simplified view would categorize marketing as a third-level purpose, below message and mission. However, when we take seriously the interactive character of Purpose Systems, the model can be even more helpful.

For example, market orientations can undergird a church's outsurge posture, its competent concern for people's needs—"felt" needs, crises, community needs. It can encourage our efforts to build bridges between belief/doctrine and life's harsh realities. Doctrine does not thrive behind barricades; it thrives when belief is connected to behavior.

By the same token, this interactive feature of Purpose Systems is a safeguard against market orientations overstepping their bounds, taking on inflated importance. This safeguard is necessary lest visitors' or prospects' "felt needs" come to define your message, lest they co-opt your Identity purposes.

Implosion

There is a well-established historical maxim that says when a group turns in on itself, the process of its self-destruction is set in motion. When this happens to individuals, psychologists may use the term implosion. In business, the expected outcome of implosion is bankruptcy. In churches, its end result is conflict dysfunction.

With rare exception, the implosion of a conflicted congregation can be dated quite specifically.

A church turns in on itself and becomes implosive when its overriding purposes and identity cease to govern choices made on less important levels.

Two results of implosion:

1. Symptoms of congregations' self-destruction surface. The church has more difficulty in coping with conflict. A conflicted atmosphere and even conflict dysfunction follow collapse of the Purpose System, not vice versa. Remember: A congregation does not get into trouble *because* of conflict. It is conflicted because more important purposes no longer make the determination in day-to-day functions and choices.

2. Lesser corporate purposes take on an inflated importance. Church management and institutional machinery concerns become too important. Budget and turfs, for instance, become divisive because members and groups lose their perspective in dealing with such matters. Personal preferences of members or cliques gain far too much influence in purpose-collapsed congregations. Two examples are:

    a) A handful of families tyrannize the congregation's vitality by using Power Play Stewardship.

    b) Members decide: "I know our pastor is doing a good job because I think he's so *nice*."

Trying to manage or resolve conflict without directly addressing a congregation's Purpose System collapse is like old King Canute trying to sweep back the sea's incoming tide with a broom.

Markers: Collapsed Purpose System

You have a Mission Statement, aided and abetted by flow charts and job descriptions. Results of your annual goal-setting retreat reflect the latest techniques. Sure, most of you feel the congregation could and should be doing much better. But, amidst all the things you are doing right, what markers or symptoms signal the probability that your corporate Body is not well and is suffering from Purpose System Collapse?

1. Nomination slates

Getting them filled has been a hassle for a long time. (The first year or so after a pastor leaves does not count.) Your most talented and busiest members have refused to accept leadership roles or give their best efforts to their present roles.

2. Back-door losses

Back-door membership losses have been a steady leak rather than a major exodus or two over the years. Some actual losses are still kept on the rolls by winking at policies set some time back. You are scrambling to stay statistically even.

3. Great goals, lousy support

It may have seemed like a great goal: a long-overdue renovation, a pipe organ, or something else supported by those who did the planning. But somebody got up at the meeting and declared: "We should be giving this money to missions, instead." Implicit in that statement is a plea: show me *how* this connects to our mission's level of importance. Goals fail unless you have worked out *why* we should support them.

4. Gossip and cliques

Without a corporate system of convincing *why's,* people will invent their own. It is called gossip. Gossip runs out of gas when it is replaced with purposeful *Whys* and *So Thats.* Cliques are little manufacturing units whose product is counterfeit Why's. They flourish in churches which slight the importance and character of their small groups, unless you have come up with convincing *purposes* for those groups.

5. Plateaued stewardship

This is a vivid marker, chronic among groups which ignore that principle we have noted: low-level purposes get low-level responses. It is not convincing to ballyhoo missions when members are not seeing *how* that claim transforms day-by-day congregational operations.

6. Evangelism: much ado about nothing

If most of your "acquisitions" are transfers rather than New Christians, that is *recruitment,* not evangelism. Going after more members instead of helping win souls for Christ is a lower purpose organizational gimmick.

7. Leadership feels more drain than gain

When leaders (pastors as well as laity) bring healthier Purpose Systems to their roles than the congregation has, that church system leeches off their emotional and spiritual reserves. Is personal growth likely in such roles? You have to be kidding!

8. Confused expectations for key people

Do you have as many different sets of expectations as you have members? For example, do all of you share the same priorities or criteria for knowing when the pastor is doing a good job? Do those criteria embody all four levels of your corporate Purpose System?

9. Battles over control

Control has its place in your Purpose System (level 3) and is a natural human craving. But is it overly noticeable at your church? Are there "strong" leaders/ groups who seem to reduce just about every issue or decision to their control agendas?

10. Obsession with rules

Is your congregation bogged down with insignificant rules regarding job descriptions and evaluations? Or, do the rules clearly express shared commitment to higher purposes? Congregations which have not figured out their own corporate Purpose System reinforce mediocrity when they evaluate individuals' performance.

11. Budget calls the shots

Nowhere does Scripture applaud fiscal jerks. But does the Budget (and its formation process) tyrannize just about everything, including stewardship? "If every giving unit would add just 21 cents per week, we could meet the budget." You never will, if meeting that budget is the main motivation. Is the Budget your power players' main weapon or are more important purposes governing your Budget's formation and use?

12. Selective care-giving

"Why should I care about Bethany when Bethany does not care about me?" Every church has a few individuals who always come through. Most churches also will respond to catastrophic need cases and to high-profile members. But can "average" members count on your *church's* purposeful support in times of personal crisis?

13. No *So Thats* in your Annual Reports
Review your last several annual reports. Are they crammed with activities, names, events, dollars-raised-and-disbursed? Or, do you see a clear sense of how these things were pulled by a vital Purpose System?

14. "We need strong leadership"
Many members are attendees only. Others on boards and committees take little initiative. "If only we could get a big strong Dog who could wag more tails around here!" But your congregation relies on *volunteers*. Under the circumstances, what most people regard as *strong* leadership is likely to undermine your Purpose System.

15. Lack of unity
When your church tries to go off in several directions at once, things start collapsing. Unity that depends on people more than on purposes is an invitation into the cult closet.

16. Outsurge by long distance
Your church can be one of the biggest givers to missions and benevolence but still be imploding and self-destructing. Is your corporate posture surging outward to those you know personally, to everyday lives through members' Monday ministries? Or, is your congregation doing most of its mission business by long distance?

If ten or more of these markers are present in your congregation, it is long overdue for intentional overhaul of its Purpose System.

Low Levels of Motivational Support

By bringing to Bethany's attention different levels of motivation for decision making, the congregation as a whole could discover a new way of setting priorities by examining the motives governing decisions.

Scripture emphasizes that levels of our motivation determine whether Conflict Redemption efforts will be eternally blessed by God or just be desirable for the church or ourselves. Here is an example of the ancient four levels of motivation:

4—*Lowest level:* If church members enter into a process of Conflict Redemption because of self-interest, personal wish-lists or mere preferences, there is no promise of eternal blessing from God. When members work out a mutually agreeable Win-Win transaction on this low personal preference motivational level, it might be nice enough, but it is not eternally *blessed.*

3—*Next level:* If church members are motivated to settle a dispute to keep peace in the family or for the good of the organization, go ahead. But in Scripture there is no promise of eternal blessing given such motives.

2—*A more important* motivation can be a church's sincere hope that people regard members' efforts as a witness-bearing Christian way of coping with conflict.

That is much better than the others, but it is not the *best* motivation.

1—*The best motivation:* God's eternal blessing upon their efforts is assured only when members enter into Conflict Redemption "unto Christ" (Matthew 18:19-20).

This highest purpose for Conflict Redemption takes a dual form:

a. We no longer regard each other from a human perspective (II Corinthians 5:17).

For church members, a change of heart between you and me follows how we see each other. "Aha! Jim, Christ has declared that you are Right with Him. So am I! On that basis, let us work on our differences." For all who are in Christ, there is a new relationship between us that overrides and surrounds our differences.

Our redemptive expectations of conflict wait upon this change of eyesight. Unless we see each other as Christ does, it will be difficult to do unto that "pain in the neck" as Christ does unto you. "Christ loves *her*? He loves the likes of *him*? I guess I am not on such shaky ground after all."

b. No longer do we strive over being Right but rather over becoming Right with each other.

Nowhere in the Bible does God promise to bless a conflictor for being right. Blessing comes only to those who are motivated to *make symphony* with each other, as unto Christ and *in* Christ. Matthew 18:19 blows all other expectations out of the water, whether Win-Win or "resolution." *Nice* expectations and *blessed* expectations are quite different. God blesses our efforts when we focus them upon making symphony in our US relationship.

What difference does it make to be *blessed* instead of merely affirmed or rewarded? Biblical doctrine on blessing is amazing: to bless is to *effect* what is affirmed. A child who lives in the confidence of parents' blessing is going to be a much happier and better-adjusted child. "Blessed are the peace-builders" encourages them into existence with the certainty of eternal expectations. ("Happy" is a perverse mistranslation for the Beatitudes, by the way.) With assurance of God's blessing when we concentrate on our One New Person needs during dissension, our agenda changes and affects prospects for a solution we dared not anticipate.

This certainty of blessing is going to change old attitudes toward our troubles from dead-end expectations and disheartened futility to a godly discontent with the way things are between us. This discontent can pull us together along the road to reconciliation within our US relationship.

Six Pathways to a Purpose System

While I provide more detailed Purpose System information in my book *Church Vitality*, there are six pathways which can be helpful.

1. Has the congregation claimed at least one Overriding Purpose?

Refer back to the list of qualifications for valid first-level purposes on page 6. Then, critique your Mission Statement, if you have one. Do not confuse objectives with purposes, because purposes include "legs" for how they will get done.

Your church may list a high priority of "saving the lost" through evangelism and assimilation. But does your kind of evangelism meet all criteria for a valid Overriding Purpose, including the participative criterion? Do your evangelism "legs" exclude participation by 90 percent of your members? If so, go back to the drawing board for a more participative mode of evangelism. Incorporate "hot call" (as known in Sales) components along with more common "cold call" versions (e.g. the Kennedy "Evangelism Explosion" program). Later, I will describe one venerable precedent for "hot call" evangelism: Christ-Care.

Before trashing existing Mission Statements and other ideas, however, move into your possible Overriding Purposes by *experience* rather than by *decree*. Live with these purposes for a year, fine-tuning how the purposes work in your congregational life. A list of principles and ingredients of Purpose Systems can be made, but each congregation has to develop its own recipe.

2. Look at whatever job descriptions or specification of tasks and responsibilities you have.

With our "No So Thats in Your Kitchen" example in mind, start comparing each specification with each of the four purpose levels for staff, boards, committees and officers. What purposes should lead the Building Committee's proposal? Too many church buildings are monuments to a collapsed Purpose System. What overriding priorities shape your expectations of the pastor? Do the congregation's levels of support for volunteers match its levels of expectation for assigned responsibilities?

Experience shows that what might look good at first glance will need repeated adjustment until it works. Bear in mind that individual members often are way ahead of the congregation's Purpose System, and you are trying to construct and implement the _latter_.

3. Move in tandem with Pathway 2 toward developing your own version of purpose-led Stewardship.

Go beyond merely listing the problem. Members already know bills have to be paid and that costs are escalating, but what they also need to know are the higher purposes which will keep those bills in perspective. (One of our sons hates to wash the car just for maintenance. But for a big date, "nooo prob-blem, Dad.")

4. Within a year, put together a three-year Vitality Strategy for the congregation.

Most churches are used to stumbling through one year at a time, fiscal fingers crossed. Others soar off into five or ten-year plans and do not live within the here and now. A three-year time frame is more realistic for most of us. If you have members accustomed to using econometrics and other management tools for strategic planning, include them in this planning process. A helpful way to pull it all together will be to fit the pieces onto a Purpose-Goals-Action continuum, our "P-G-A Principle" (see page 19).

5. "PEG" the congregation.

Vital leadership, unity, direction and the whole atmosphere of your church depend on your Purpose Embodiment Groups.

PEGS
(Purpose Embodiment Groups)

For specialists in ideological movements and language, such as C. S. Lewis, small groups "PEG" the whole movement and heavily determine its actual character and dynamics. PEG means: Purpose Embodiment Groups, which are constituted around a vital system of purposes. If there are no clear purposes bonding a group at church, it can turn into a gossip clique.

Small group concepts are a dime-a-dozen these days. Many claim to be modeled after the Early Church. Most of them also either fizzle out quickly or drift off on to the Conventicle fringe (become schismatic). Unlike small groups which are affinity-based, organized around "felt needs," or activity-oriented, a PEG binds together around purposes. Specifically, it embodies the Purpose System of the larger church (not merely of that congregation). It is like a *cell* which contains all the genetic material of the larger Body. Although the communist version may come to mind, both the image and reality long preceded Marx.

In order to cut through the small group rhetoric, it may be helpful to use the PEG/Cell model as a benchmark for evaluating any small group theory. Then, we can get back to much better-informed and faithful adaptations of the *original* versions! Back through the Norwegian mission movement, Classic Pietism, the Wesleys, to the Apostolic church itself, PEG's have anchored the Church. (PEG's are detailed in our books *Church Vitality* and *Christ-Care*.)

6. *Where* **your church is headed (Goals) and** *how* **you will get there (Actions) are going to be decided and supported by** *why* **(Purposes) you are going there.**

How (Action) you are going to get there depends upon those purposes and goals. It is a continuum, flowing in both directions: Purposes-Goals-Actions, or P-G-A.

P-G-A Principle
(Purpose-Goals-Action)

The ship had gone dead in the water, while up on deck passengers and crew argued over its destination.

"New York City! I want to see the Big Apple."

"Oslo! I am dying for some good lutefisk."

"No, London! There are some wonderful new shows this season in the West End."

"Calcutta! Why? Because famine rages there and our holds are full of food."

Anyone who knows Scripture and also knows how things get done in Monday's world realizes the importance of goal-setting. But few of us understand why *corporate* goals, especially in the church, often end up in some file cabinet. Most often, it is because the church does not work out *why* that goal is worth supporting or achieving. Show us its *so that* connections with what we are all about.

"We should be giving that money to Missions, instead!" usually is as much a question as a declaration. In effect: "Show me *why* this pipe organ project is as important for us as Missions." Even though you might raise enough dollars for that organ, if you cannot show members *why*, it will remain a divisive factor for years to come.

That brings up another quandary: stewardship and financial support. There is another corollary to the principle noted earlier: *higher purposes bring higher responses.* Most contributors to television evangelism empires were members of congregations like yours, whose rhetoric floats lofty ideals but whose nitty-gritty is captive to *low* purposes, low So Thats.

If you say, "If every giving unit gave 28 cents a week more, we would make the budget!" you will fail, and not only because calling me a *giving unit* is demeaning. If meeting the budget is all there is, why should the rest of us take heed? Such bean-counting approaches reinforce an already pervasive impression about your congregation, that it is bogged down in self-interest and institutional self-preservation.

P-G-A illustrates the difference between commonplace Mission Statement methodologies and how you make use of an effective Purpose System. Indeed, P-G-A becomes a measure of your purpose's validity. If your specified purposes do not mesh well with your goals and action plan, take another hard look at those purposes. Specified goals also have to face continuing scrutiny from your purposes and action plan perspectives. P-G-A works like that basic biblical theme recurring throughout this book: making symphony.

Distinguishing *Most* from *Least:* with a collapsed Purpose System, everything becomes equally important, so nothing is really important. Every little thing becomes grounds for blowing up. But in a vital Purpose System, things can be kept in perspective.

Fourth Monday Night

Throughout my childhood, we had to leave the house those Monday nights every other month. All I was told was: "Because Immanuel is coming over to talk with Dad." My father had no known allergies but would break out in hives around Immanuel, head of the Deacons the entire 22 years Dad was pastor at Zion.

I was nine years old the night I sneaked back into the house to find out why I was not supposed to be there. Hiding under the stairway, unknown to my father, I could watch and hear what happened. The doorbell rang.

"Good evening, Doctor Qualben."

"Good evening, Immanuel." *Very* formal and stiff. I hardly dared to breathe. Seated facing each other, in two worn easy chairs, Immanuel looked at Dad,

"Let us pray, pastor." And he began with phrases I was quite used to. Except there came forth pleas such as: "Yeesus, send thy Holy Spirit to open hardened hearts with us here tonight." Dad was the only other person there! (That was my first time hearing prayer used as a dive-bombing attack.) Well, in *his* prayer, Dad nailed Immanuel right back. I figured it was a Draw.

Immanuel took out slips of paper from various pockets: complaints about their pastor which members had "brought to my attention." The litany began. Level 4 stuff: forgotten names, slights, and the like. Dad's interpersonal skills could be spotty at times. I did not like the edge to their voices, with Immanuel's irresistable force meeting my father's immovable object (a.k.a. Stubborn Norwegian).

Another set of complaints, this time about my Dad's deficiencies in Parish Administration. "Pastor, they are saying you are spending too much time in the study. You got to visit the people more." Arguing ensued (because this church was in the mission movement heritage of continental Pietism which required a scholar-pastor.) But there came the other complaint: "Pastor, you have to spend more time in the Study because they are saying it is hard to get ahold of you." (You just can't win, I thought.

Years later, I found out Dad had sent into Synod the same set of statistics seven years in a row. Indeed, after he was killed, his successor found hundreds more active members than Dad had reported to Minneapolis.) But by this time, I was terrified: I was witnessing my father *losing his job!* I would become a *waif* because of this, wandering from door to door begging for handouts! (I had been reading a "Classic Comic" that day, *Tale of Two Cities,* and waif was in there.) Loud arguing. Impasse.

Then...it all changed. "Pastor? Missus So-and-So" (I cannot recall her name) "is going around Zion telling people that because her conversion was so Big, her interpretation of the Scriptures is just as good as Dr. Qualben's. Now then, Pastor, we have to *stop* her from this!" It was as though the Indians had suddenly turned into the Wagons, drawing into a circle around the Pastor. (Zion's Identity purposes had come under attack, in other words.) Now, something much more important than all the other stuff was at stake. And, both men knew it. "If we cannot stop this, the mission of Zion is done for!" Immanuel said.

When they had agreed on how to handle that problem, another hour was devoted to the obviously most important part of the evening: talking over Christ-care (Luther's phrase) situations. Who was doing what; how was it going; what else needs to be done?

Then came the only time I ever heard Dad speak in Norwegian voluntarily: they prayed together, when the rest was finished. I did not understand any of it. But what was happening, I will never forget. One spoke a line or two, the other came into the prayer; back and forth. I was watching two saints making symphony prayer, joining together, in harmony addressing their beloved Lord as the God He is instead of as some spiritual Go-fer.

After my Dad was killed, Gordon (another Deacon) spelled out for me how it was with Immanuel and Dad. Oh yes, they fought and argued. But *only* over matters they—and the rest of active Zion—knew were "less important" things. On the highest two Purpose levels, they stood together—bonded—against all threats to "The Mission!" That reality which overrode all else at Zion, which pulled it all together was my first vivid experience with how a church's vital purpose system actually *works*.

We may speak of Purpose Systems. As readily, we could use the phrase Purpose Symphony among ourselves—key recurring themes interacting with other themes. One theme may deliberately diminish in the others' favor for a time before soaring again. But always in symphony, harmoniously.

Afterword

Without exception, every troubled or plateaued congregation I have worked with or know of either lost or never had a decisive "system" of *So Thats* pulling everything that church is about. When these So Thats are lacking, not only does conflict become inevitable, but other ingredients in your conflict's recipe will defy solution. Collapse of your congregation's Purpose System costs far too much. Not only does it render your church incapable of knowing when anybody (pastor included) is doing a good job, but collapsed So Thats cripple volunteer motivation, evangelism and stewardship. This soil provides ideal growing conditions for power plays and control games.

On the other hand, reliance on your specific Purpose System is a key to church vitality. It transforms bonding mechanisms throughout the congregation, leadership, decisions and expectations, while building durable unity.

2

Purposeful Reliance on Doctrine

---◻︎---

"If our doctrine does not work between you and me, it stops working between God and me!"

When I said these words to a Texas congregation,
a member jumped to his feet and yelled:
"Heresy!"
Surprised, I tried to say *"But Christ said...."*
He blurted out *"Sola Fide! Justi-fi-ca-shun by faith
alone! It has nothing to do with my brother!"*
I tried again saying *"But Christ said..."*
He bellowed, *"Then Christ must have been **wrong!**"*

A true story and unfortunately so typical of Christians in America who regard religion as a strictly private matter. Maybe it can be private if you have sold out to that Maharishi fellow, but not if you are a Christian and have an interest in heaven. What would have happened if the Apostles had considered their religion a private matter?

In the clear testimony of Christ in Scripture, people are playing games with their eternal destiny by failing to do unto others as Christ does unto us. This is especially tempting at church whenever we get so carried away during a disagreement that everything we stand for flies out the window.

Bridging Belief and Behavior

Our church systems come unglued at the very center when we do not practice our doctrine. Behavioral betrayal of doctrine generates negative evangelism, discouraging many from hearing the doctrine we *declare* but do not *do* in our congregational and denominational life. My personal fuse gets shortest in the presence of purveyors of pure doctrine who fail to live out that doctrine in their everyday life. As they wallow in church politics, finesse a convention election, or betray the authority of Scripture, they would mock God in orthodoxy's defense.

Why is this so common and why are so many churches blind to how much offense it gives?

The miracle of Christian life is that we are right with God while still sinners (*simul iustus et peccator*). That same miracle is just as certain for the Church's life as for mine. A Christian congregation, corporately, is the same kind of mixed bag any Christian person is—feet of clay and crown of glory; simultaneously! Held together in a tension sustained solely by God's grace. Amazing! A Miracle!

In your congregation, there is a *Body of Christ* character and there is its *institutional* life: righteous while sinner. As with our personal life in Christ, both aspects

are inseparable. These aspects are distinct, but not separate, lest we imagine there is a dualism about the church
which filters the good from the bad parts, or separates
good guys from bad guys, true-blue saints from sinners,
real disciples from mere members.

Every congregation is in a wheat-and-tares situation. As Christ emphasized in that parable, deciding
which is which does not become our business since God
will separate them at the final harvest.

A first step toward coping with our corporate be-
trayals of belief is to bless the church's hybrid nature. It
is a hybrid of saintly and sinful, a hybrid system of Body
and Institution: a "system" whose earthly *persona* merits
much more than mere tolerance.

When I get disgusted with the church's institutional
absurdities, faults and bureaucratic self-interest, I am
sorely tempted to give up. Then, I remember that this
church-life quandary is the very same one going on
between God and me. My prayer is not for God to
demolish my sinful nature, but rather that His grace in
Christ will abound all the more *so that* I can live and
work in this hybrid church of His by that same grace.

Nothing in this book should be construed to dis-
criminate between "super-dooper" Christians (a.k.a.
Disciples) and "lazybone" Christians (a.k.a. those "Barely
inside the Kingdom"). Each of us is a mix of both sorts.
So is the church. *Peace in the Parish* is intended for the
whole hybrid, mixed-bag status of any Christian and
any Christian congregation. *Christian* insofar as we
claim and bless the miracle that, through God's grace,
we are at once righteous and sinful.

BELIEF AT WORK

So many Christians are far more effective in putting what they believe to work in their personal lives than they are in their church. One result of this dichotomy is that few congregations emphasize *doing* doctrine in how things get run. O yes, rules do abound, but those rules' relation to a church's doctrine are often far-fetched, at best.

What is the culprit? Probably the way we teach and learn doctrine in our churches. When our pedagogical principle amounts to a conceptual chauvinism, truths link with truths rather than with life. The Reformers' "What does this mean?" loses its purposeful commerce with reality, its "How does this work?" emphasis.

For example:
- Do we live and work together in that same forgiveness we beg God for in our personal prayer life?
- In going about our church tasks, do the same motivations work there that each of us seek in our personal Christian sense of vocation? Do the same concerns direct our church relationships that inspire what we want our Christian marriage or family to become?

In *principle,* it is not difficult to align congregational governance with personal Christian experience because a congregation is much more than the sum of its members; it has its own *persona* or person-hood. Let us begin by taking that personal-corporate correlation of aspirations as our starting point for developing a purposeful reliance on doctrine.

Personally and corporately, we probably have more desire than substance when it comes to putting our belief to work. One key to turning this around is to reorient group Bible study to connect Head and Heart, Faith and Works, Truth and Life. To argue over which is more important is like debating which scissor blade is more important when both are needed to cut it. We need to go back and forth asking: What does this *mean?* How does this *work?* For what *purpose?*

We also need to:

- Avoid reducing the Heart/Work component to mere application of a text or verse because this kind of application collapses down to moralism and trivial activity.

- Keep Bible study *purposeful.* Consider vital questions such as:

  1. What does this text do to the way we see each other? *So that* what greater blessing can be ours?

  2. How does this text open my eyes to what is really happening in a particular area of my life's landscape? So that I can see God's face turned toward me *there?*

  3. How does the doctrine of this text equip me to cope redemptively with a troubling relationship? How can all of my relationships be nourished by the healing power of God's Word?

Such questions are examples of how we move beyond dreary Insights-Application approaches (the Bible Study Two-Step) to become at home *within* God's Word.

Purposeful Bible study is one piece in the pattern of growth in faith literacy. This growth is necessary because:

  1. A congregation widens the gap between corporate belief and behavior unless members go back to the

drawing board and re-think how congregational groups or systems make and deliver choices.

2. Commitment to make our shared message decisive has to become our way of doing things in our daily lives and in our congregation. This commitment is not merely a reassembly task, as though we could tear down a Hyundai and create a Porsche from its parts.

3. Our belief will be little more than a fervently-saluted flag unless and until it *governs* our systems, functions, choices and fellowship.

Purposeful reliance on doctrine is one of Conflict Redemption's three principles. As an introduction to this approach to experienced biblical teaching, I have used the following as a format and sequence for Bible class presentations on "How Does Doctrine Work?" During an on-site consultation such a presentation is a major factor for many members in authorizing the Conflict Redemption process.

How Does Doctrine *Work?*

Beloved in Christ, God knows all about you but loves you nonetheless!

But how can that *be?* There are so many differences left unsettled between God and me. There is so much *conflict* in my relationship with God. How can God know all about me but love *me* nonetheless?

Christian life stands upon being right with God while yet a sinner still in conflict with Him. God created that right relationship with Him even before we could settle our differences.

The way God deals with us is such a radical contrast with how we deal with each other. We insist on settling our differences as the basis for restoring a right relationship. "If I can get what I deserve out of this, we can get back together again." We make reconciliation a transaction.

God does not deal with us that way. He does not come to me and say: "Jim, there are a lot of things about you I do not like. When you have shaped up, give me a call. Meanwhile, keep in touch." That would amount to salvation by works righteousness!

How different God's way is from *our* way! God declares to me: "You are *mine*. Because of Christ, things are right between us! On *that* basis, let us get to work on our differences. Although you are never going to shape up on all of these things, never forget this: you are mine! Things *are* right between us." There is no transaction, only the gift of making me His own.

In the midst of conflict between God and me, redemption does happen. New life is created, although the strife never ends. Christians: *it is okay to have conflict!* It is okay so long as we expect the same kind of redemption to come of it as comes out of conflict between God and you. In order to better understand how our relationship with God models our relationship with each other, let us consider the doctrines of:

- **Grace**
- **Love**
- **Righteousness**
- **Forgiveness**

Grace

Yes, grace works between you and me the same way it works between God and you: we are reconciled with each other in the face of many differences which just do not go away. That same grace of God we live by begins to work among us when we *see* each other in Christ through God's eyes.

Christian living has as much to do with a change of *eyes* as with a change of *heart*. When I see *you* as someone whom God has declared as His own, and if you see *me* the same way, how we treat each other can never again be the same.

Buster

The first time I found out how Grace works was in eighth grade. Buster was one of the most obnoxious people I had ever met. He was so obnoxious you wanted to hit him one, just on general principle.

Since I am one of those preacher's kids, some of you may not be surprised to hear that I instigated a coalition of myself, Herbie and Charlie. The objective was to punch- bag Buster as a reminder of how little we appreciated him. Each of us was a specialist: Herbie was the best fighter in school, Charlie knew about hitting Buster only where he had clothes on; otherwise, we would leave marks. I was the brains of this outfit.

Noon recess that Thursday was B-Day. As the three of us lurked, ready and waiting for Buster's return from lunch at home, something very strange happened. Buster's father brought him back from recess. His father was influential in local politics and a bit of a hero to us kids. It was rumored that he had forced the city to roll back pool fees to nine cents from the announced 26 cents. He helped get the Board of Education to reopen school yards after school so we could play stick ball there instead of out in the streets dodging cars.

Buster's father brought him to the school yard gate. Then it happened. He gave Buster a hug, ruffled his hair with affection and, with a laughing swat on his backside, sent him on into school! My jaw dropped.

"*He* loves...*Buster*?" Impossible! But I had just seen it with my own eyes! In effect, our punch bag trio saw the man display a very certain message: "This kid is *mine*. I love him. Do not forget that!"

Buster never changed. He stayed as obnoxious as ever until I lost track of him sometime during college years. But how I *treated* Buster changed. Every time I felt like lashing out at him, I saw that scene with his father: "This kid is *mine*!" My eyes had changed. How I *saw* Buster changed how I treated him. This beloved was the only child of a father the rest of us admired.

Who is *your* "Buster" these days? Try seeing your Buster from God's point of view. Does that mean you also have to *love* this Buster?

I never came to love Buster as a brother. Yet, Christ does command us to "love one another as I have loved you." Indeed, He made it one of the church's three main objectives, to embody God's compassionate love in Christ.

Love

What is this love of Christ, this same love which caused God to give His only Son so that His creation would be restored to what He had intended? It is not brotherly love, not its parental and family version; surely not married or romantic love; neither is it tough love, nor that voluptuous love of chocolates. God was not feeling *nice* about the world at Golgatha. *Agape,* the Greek word we have heard of so often does not help much either, since it was only a vague translation from the original word used by our Lord and the disciples.

RAHAMIM LOVE

To help clear up our confusion about Love, consider the word Jesus actually used. The Hebrew/Aramaic word is *rahamim* (pronounced rah-ha-MEEM). In the Bible *rahamim* literally means the "uterus of God Almighty."

That is the picture in Isaiah, where God declares that He has carried Israel as a mother carries her unborn child. Without going into all the details which biblical rabbis taught from this word-picture, we can summarize its main points.

1. New life (the "Prince of Peace") is created in God's *rahamim* from conflict itself.

2. The birth of this Prince of Peace from the *rahamim* of God guarantees the eventual reconciliation of all conflicts throughout the universe.

3. With His birth the Love of God becomes incarnate.

This is mind-boggling imagery, but it conveys the core meaning underlying what Christ taught about Love. *Christian love nourishes and restores life in our relationships,* even among people in a congregation. Pain often accompanies this love, but this is the same kind of pain which happens in childbirth—intense but blessed, because it is associated with new life. Christian *life-birthing* love nourishes that life and sees to its best.

God "so *rahamims* the world" that, in sending His only Son, He restores that world back to redeemed life with Him.

The Samaritan has compassionate love (*rahamim*) upon a half-dead man lying by the side of the road, and the man is restored to life.

Christ has *rahamim* toward Lazarus, and this dead brother of Mary and Martha strides forth from the tomb *laughing* exuberantly.

The Waiting Father has *rahamim* toward his Prodigal Son, even while the young man was yet far off. Their dead relationship is brought back to life so robustly that the sounds of merry-making annoy that nit picking elder brother out in the fields.

One New Person Relationship

As with living by grace, Christian love is *purposeful*, "So That" love. We love as Christ loves when our actions happen *so that* the best things will come to a relationship and will strengthen, renew or even revive it.

We love as Christ does when our choice of action is focused on our *relationship*, whether it is with our children, spouse, church members or co-workers. This is so different from ordinary loves, which focus either on the other person or on yourself. Christian love is led by purposeful *so thats* for the sake of the relationship God created for both or all of you. Whether you decide to "give in" or "say no," we embody Christ's love when our decision is made for the sake of our One New Person relationship.

What makes a relationship *Christian*? What makes a marriage *Christian*? What makes a family, friendship,

vocation or church *Christian*? Is ours a Christian home
because of what we all do or do not do? Is there
something more basic than that? For insights and
answers about the essence of Christian relationships,
we need to consider another biblical doctrine from a
purposeful perspective.

Righteousness

Emphasis on putting the doctrine of righteousness
to work often becomes an invitation to deadly legalism.
People regard righteousness as a *goal* rather than being
the *home* where we dwell in Christ. But we are not home
alone. Religion is not the private matter between Me-
and-God that most biblical illiterates think it is. Putting
this doctrine to work *purposefully* opens some of the
most creative experiences possible for Christians.

God has said of you and me, "You are mine!" *So
that*...what? So that our relationships are transformed,
for one thing. Some of the best known righteousness
passages in the New Testament are linked with three
themes:

- **new creation**
- **relationships**
- **compassionate love**

A New Creation

In II Corinthians 5:17ff, we hear that when we no
longer regard life from a non-Christian perspective, we
see that "if anyone is in Christ, there is a new creation."
In this passage, Paul takes a contemporary rabbinic
teaching about righteous creations and centers it in
Christ.

When we pick up on that, it becomes very interesting because this theme connects these verses to one of Paul's major teachings throughout Ephesians, centered in Chapter 2:10-16. Paul's insight into the character of Christian relationships looks like this: In Christ, God brings Jew and Gentile together and creates "in himself, from the two: One New Person." So what?

One New Person Relationship

We now know that this One New Person is:
   a) bigger-than-both-of-us, and
   b) a living, breathing, distinct "person."

We are a body (as in Body of Christ); a complex organism (as in vine-and-branches). This is a *new creation* of God's doing, a person which exceeds the sum of its previous parts. In other words, when He creates a living Christian *relationship,* it is as if God brings two dimes together to make a quarter.

To call a marriage *Christian* is to see that it is living within its birthright. It is more than a partnership, more than a merger or contract. It is a One New Person. A *righteous US,* as Paul's teacher Gamaliel is said to have taught. Now we can begin to see why a Christian wedding is a *creation* service.

The same source and birthright defines and describes our *other* One New Person relationships: the Christian Family, Vocation, Neighbor, Friendship, Citizen (remember Romans 13), and Body of Christ. Each "US" (a synonym for One New Person) is more than the sum of its parts and is a living creature, *not* some mere concept.

My Vocation *One New Person* is much more than me-and-my-job-and-workplace, for example. So also, the Body of Christ of your congregation is more than your membership roll and assets, more than the organization.

Christian Love's Objective is an US!

These righteous new creation relationships are the lives which are nourished and nurtured by our *rahamim* love, that compassion in action. Remember those biblical examples we cited earlier—Lazarus, the Good Samaritan and the Prodigal Son. In each instance, a One New Person relationship was nourished, restored or created by Christian love.

Add to that list a tragic example from the Parable of the Unmerciful Servant at the end of Matthew 18. The employer had compassion on the servant's Vocation US and forgave an enormous debt. But that ingrate devoured it for himself, diverting it from his Vocation US, thereby canceling the employer's compassion.

PURPOSEFUL RELIANCE ON RIGHTEOUSNESS

Now we can discern *purposeful* reliance on Righteousness. Why? *So that* others bonded with you to that One New Person are no longer *objects* but the same *subject* with you. Righteous new creations are *so that* our One New Persons are on the receiving end of *our doing unto our US as Christ has done unto you.*

If we do not discern the Body of Christ or another One New Person, forgiveness deteriorates into a trans-

action between two egos and quickly becomes counterfeit. A One New Person relationship means we can now
enter into forgiveness *for the sake* of our marriage or
family or Body of Christ "US," before we feel quite
ready. On that foundation, we get on with living in forgiveness, healing of memories, and the rest of it.

Enter, the Deceiver! Trouble, distress and conflict
come. What happens? The Deceiver (e.g. Genesis 3)
turns these distresses into veils which conceal a One
New Person from us. Trouble blinds us to the US that
God already created. Satan piles layer upon layer, until
our One New Person starts to suffocate, getting weaker
from our distraction and neglect. Obsession with issues
starts torturing that US relationship. What loves do
remain no longer include *rahamim*, the basic food for any
US.

Enter the Peace of God: Conflict Redemption's agenda
concentrates on peeling off each blinding and suffocating layer of what has gone wrong. Why? *So that* our US
can revive, breathe again, take nourishment and grow
again. That righteous new creation which God created
and to which He bonded us comes back to life. When we
see and experience once more what God has accomplished and is doing in our life even now, *that* is what the
Bible means by the "Peace of God." God's peace is a *deja
vu* experience: our "Aha! This has already happened to
US. Now we see what you are doing, Lord!"

If our purposeful reliance on doctrine does not focus
on our personal relationships, our personal forgiveness
will be cancelled by Almighty God (Matthew 18:35, for
example). So much of that purposeful reliance hinges
upon forgiving and forgetting.

Forgiveness

There is so much counterfeit forgiveness in so many forms. Most often it happens because our purposes are phony.

- "I forgive you. Now get out of here!" (Dismissal Forgiveness)
- "I forgive you. Now are you happy?" (Insincere Forgiveness)
- "I forgive you. So can I get the new dishwasher?" (Transaction Forgiveness)
- "I forgive you. You have been drinking again, poor baby. But you know I will forgive you." (Enabler Forgiveness)
- "I forgive you. But I will *never* let you forget it!" (Power-Shark Forgiveness)

Not even the alcoholic's spouse version of enabling is genuine forgiveness because none of it happened so that an US relationship would be strengthened. All are ego transaction forgiveness, and that is why they are counterfeit.

Power Shark forgiveness is even tougher because we are not very good at forgetting. Some parents even tell their children: "If you forgive him, do not ever let him forget it because that is your lock on him from now on, your key to power." Even when we do forgive heartily and in good faith for the sake of our One New Person, we still have trouble with that *forgetting* part.

There is more to it than personal failure to forget, however. I believe that the past is Satan's chief weapon against most Christian relationships. The past is so powerful, it keeps tens of thousands of psychiatrists in business! We build time bombs whenever we get sloppy and just shrug off the past with inane statements:

> "Well, time will heal all wounds."
> "Let's just bury the hatchet."
> "Let's look at the past as prologue."
> "Let's all agree we will not bring up the past anymore."

You know how powerful the past can become. You are growing as a Christian until this voice comes from somewhere. "Some Christian *you* are. Don't you remember what you did when you were sixteen?" You reply: "But that was *forgiven!*" That sneering voice hits you again: "I know that. But don't you *remember?*" Score another grand slam for that ancient Accuser!

The past also participates in the church's present. Trying to "resolve" conflicted issues which have strong roots in the past is like pulling up a tuft of Creeping Jenny grass. You think you got it all, only to find the same plant popping up elsewhere in your lawn via its hidden root system. Maybe the presenting issue was what *they* did to a former pastor who had meant so much to your family during a time of crisis. Maybe it was what was said to you during a building program debate. The past is running amok, and with that, we have handed Satan more deadly ammunition.

The Accuser's target: amok means "in a frenzy to kill." To kill what? What is Satan's favorite killing target? One of our God-created US relationships!

FORGETTING

When it comes to things that have happened, ordinary forgetting is hard to do. All of us have moments of forgetfulness about items on our *To Do* lists, times when we are preoccupied or emotionally over-saturated. For some people, intense guilts and old hurts can so overload our memory banks that timely response to another's pressing need gets postponed. "I just cannot handle any more," we convince ourselves.

Before the printing press, people had a more sophisticated view of memory and its uses than we do. It was a key part of "giving the birthright," for example, as when Jacob supplanted Esau. Receiving Isaac's memory gave Jacob authority, while inheriting his property only would have provided a livelihood. For us, however, Scripture provides more pertinent and profound insights as well as how-to's for the *redemption* of memories.

The Bible fully understands how the past and future participate in our present lives and relationships. (This is why a Hebrew word for remember, *zakhor*, is used in a masculine sense—to specify how past or future events "act upon" us now.) Hence, the biblical doctrine of forgetting specifically targets the often devastating impacts of participatory time in our lives. How so?

BIBLICAL KEYS TO OUR PAST

Time is participative—When the Psalmist pleads, "Remember not the sins of my youth, O Lord," he is asking that God will not allow the impacts of his sins to *participate* in his life now.

God's name is Time-Participative—God's holiest name, JHWH in Hebrew and Alpha-Omega in Greek, can be translated as the Lord of Participatory Time. The Lord of how the Past and Future "participate" in our lives right *now*.

"Remembrance" in Scripture focuses on who is Lord of the Past's participatory power in our lives: you, me, or God?

"Remember" happens when something from the Past or Future participates in the Present—according to the Bible. God "remembers His Covenant" blessing for thousands of generations and the blessings are truly present in each generation. "Do this for My remembrance" means our Lord's life, death and resurrection are no mere fond memory.

Biblical "forgetting" is at the heart of Israel's most sacred day (Day of Atonement: *Yom Kippur*) and of Christ's constitution of the church's ministry (e.g. John 20:20-23 and Matthew 18:18). In Scripture, Forgive-and-Forget are not distinct actions but two sides of the same coin. We see this vividly expressed in the Day of Atonement service of Leviticus 16. First, a bull is sacrificed for God's forgiveness of Israel's sins. Then, a goat is brought out. Aaron, the High Priest, takes the complete list of those just-forgiven sins and *binds* those sins to the goat's forehead. Whereupon, the goat is led off so far into the wilderness ("to a place cut off" the text says) as to be hopelessly lost. Why? So that the deadly power of those forgiven sins cannot return, cannot be *remembered,* cannot participate in Israel's on-going life.

Each year, on the Day of Atonement, Israel claimed God's Almighty work of forgiveness *and* forgetting. An

overlooked but important point was that as Aaron performed the bull and goat rituals, Israel realized that
neither Aaron nor those actions actually caused or created the forgiveness-forgetting. An easily overlooked
grammatical technicality (use of the future perfect periphrastic construction also in Matthew 18:18 and John
20:23) makes clear that the real Doer is God. It means
that when, *in* Christ I forgive you, God will have already
forgiven you. When I claim God's power to forget that
thing, God will have already *bound* its killing power to
the moment of forgiveness.

God's action of forgetting separates us from a forgiven sin's participatory power as far as East is from
West. "I have buried it in the depths of the sea, " God
declares. When tempting us to take back control of that
thing, Satan is saying: "in the deepest part of the sea,
huh? Come on, let's go *fishing.*"

Christian *forgetting* is far less a memory matter than
it is a decision over lordship. Whenever we do not let go
of it or give up control over its participatory power, the
sin or hurt we would forgive is *not* forgiven *in God's
name.* So long as we do it in *our* name and under our
control, it is phony forgiveness.

My own past becomes a poison pill stuck in my craw
as long as I hold over you that supposedly forgiven
thing from our past. You know such people: bitter,
mean, chronic scapegoat addicts, souls shriveling up
like prunes from the heat of old hurts clutched in clenched
fists. When we hold on to hurts, the rest of our past
becomes the killing field of guilt.

But if I let go of those hurts, hand over lordship to our
Alpha-Omega, my past will start turning into the green
pastures of assurance and peace. I might recall what

happened and even recall its trauma and hurt. But now it is powerless and can no longer be in a frenzy to kill an US relationship.

FIVE STEPS TO FORGIVEN LIFE TOGETHER

How do we go about this? I would suggest five practical steps.

Step 1. Commit yourselves to healing the real wounds rather than putting band-aids on surface scratches.

The more severe the hurt, the more likely we are to overlay it with survival camouflages. A common survival camouflage for adult survivors of childhood sex abuse, for example, is to ascribe fault to someone who is less emotionally traumatizing than an abusive relative. To enter into a forgiveness strategy which would name only superficial substitutes leaves the real wound untouched and festering.

As each camouflage layer is pulled aside, expect that another long-hidden layer will be less terrifying than you once thought it would be. The light at the end of your tunnel now shines more brightly on that layer.

Step 2. Focus on whatever One New Person relationships are most directly jeopardized by this past wound.

Make that US relationship your *so that* focus. For example, for the sake of your marriage relationship build a forgiveness foundation upon which the rest of your forgiveness experience can be built. In other words, do not wait until you *feel* forgiving or are *ready* to do so.

Step 3. Understand biblical teaching on forgiveness and forgetting, lest you set yourself up for counterfeit versions and expectations.

This probably means some rather basic revisions in your previous understanding of these things. Why? Because we Americans have been addicted to reading Scripture through privatistic prisms that block out the personal relationship cradle in which much of biblical doctrine is laid. Christianity is personal but never private.

Another aspect of this third step is to become familiar enough with the pathways and principles of Matthew 18:15-20 so that you will confidently rely on this passage for your personal relationships no less than for its church use.

Step 4. Be clear about your *so thats* in how you sequence repenting and forgiving.

How important must repentance be prior to restoring a forgive/forget relationship? When should forgiveness precede "shaping up" and become its healing foundation? One helpful key for making this difficult decision is to view the best repentance-and-forgiveness sequence from a *so that* perspective: *so that* what can happen?

Step 5. Strengthen your forgive-and-forget bond through ritual settings.

My wife puts it well: "It is nice to hear you say 'I love you,' but it goes down so much better over candlelight." Ritual, after all, emphasizes blessed surprise. That blessed surprise of getting what we do not deserve, such as the blessed surprise of the Gospel. Others can play with ordinary forgiving transactions. Christian forgiveness defies deserving; it is etched in the genre of surprise.

You might think it is sufficient to just say "I forgive you." Maybe that will stick. It is even more important to connect it with the much more difficult forgetting part via appropriate ritual. (Note: ritual and liturgy are not co-equal. Too much of today's liturgy is poor ritual.) Go to your church sanctuary, the two (or more) of you. Perhaps you could use one of the *Bond of Peace Service* examples shown in Chapter 15. How much you make of the occasion probably will hinge on how much need you feel there is for it. But do bless and strengthen the renewal and uplifting of your relationship through ritual components which work for both of you.

Making Symphony

Is making symphony considered a biblical doctrine? Paul kept emphasizing the need to harmonize our various doctrines to keep them in symphony in our lives. At least, it is a theme-thread woven through the major doctrines we have heard. It is a key to any biblically-faithful agenda for Christian relationships. We have overlooked it for too long.

Symphoneisosin (Matthew 18:19; also Luke 14:29) "If two of you make symphony," focus conflict redemption efforts on your *relationship* more than on the issues, more than on ego needs. That is when God blesses those efforts. Nowhere does God's Word promise His eternal blessing for our games of who is *right* or *wrong*. In Conflict Redemption, our purposeful reliance on doctrine is so that we will *make symphony* in one or more of our God-given US relationships.

It is nice to agree. But that is not the Bible's main objective for coping with conflict.   Agree, resolve, manage: all these miss the point for Christians. The chronic mistranslation of Matthew 18:19 ("agree") has been misleading, aiding and abetting intellectual constipation which besets too many members of the Body. I was eleven years old when I had my first run-in with this mistranslation.

My Blue Columbia Bike

As a preacher's kid and the youngest of three sons, most things I got were hand-me-downs. By the time I got my first tricycle, it no longer had a seat or pedals so I used it as a three-wheel scooter. By 11, I was anxious to get a two-wheeler. Paul had gotten a used one and eventually handed it down to Phil. After it had been run over by a truck, dear old Phil said "Here, Jimmy, it's yours."   What to do? My problem-solving skills were acute but not always on target in those days.

My friend Vinnie was also in dire need of a two-wheeler. His mother was on welfare and no more able to cough up the cash than my family could. My first sure-fire plan for the two of us: sell Burpee seeds via one of those comic book ads. Neighbors began asking Dad if I was all right. I was trying to sell them corn seed—in New York City! In the meantime, Vinnie and I kept dropping by the bike shop: We had chosen **them:** mine, a splendid blue Columbia; Vinnie's, a red Schwinn.

One Sunday morning I was actually *listening* to my father reading the Gospel text. It was Matthew 18:15-20. Bikes were on my mind. Then I heard **the**

solution: "If two of you agree on anything you shall ask, God will give it to you" that mistranslation said. I could hardly wait for church to end. Bible in hand, I ran and banged on Vinnie's door.

"We're gonna get our bikes! It's right here!" I showed him that verse. Vinnie responded with "You're crazy." "Vinnie, my father says that if you cannot trust God's Word, you can't trust anything." My powers of persuasion got down to making a deal with Vinnie.

For the next ten school days, we sat on our back stoops after school. I had made up two cards. One said: "Dear Lord, you have said that when two of us agree on anything we ask, you will give it to us. I need a blue Columbia bike, model so-and-so." (I wanted to make sure God would get it right.) "And Vinnie here agrees with me. Don't you, Vinnie!" Added was a big "AMEN" which I shoved in front of Vinnie for him to say aloud. He read from a similar card with his bike information and got my "AMEN."

Ten days later, Vinnie grumbled that we were no closer to our bikes "than when we started this foolishness." I feared he was right and went into my first crisis of faith. Could we trust God's Word? I was so crushed that I signed up on my father's counseling list.

Dad took me into his office. I explained what had happened, heartbroken and wondering why God had not zapped me with lightning during last night's storm. Dad's first response? "Well, Jimmy, that's what you get for praying with a Catholic!" But then he went over to his books and took out the Greek New Testament. Studying but for a moment, he looked at me. "Jimmy, it says *symphoneisosin*, not agree." He explained, and I felt so relieved.

Three weeks later, as I neared Zion on Sunday morning, I noticed lots of angry-looking deacons and trustees pointing at the front page of the *Staten Island Advance*. Naive, I walked into church and was confronted by the head of our deacons. "Yaymss! Come with me!" I knew I was in big trouble with that "Yaymss!"

He led me into a room chock full of angry Norwegians. My father was jabbing his finger at the *Advance*. "Jaymsss!" he scowled, "explain this." There it was, the other part of my deal with Vinnie. Three columns wide, bottom right hand corner, front page: "Dr. Qualben's Son Wins K. of C. Drawing."

For Vinnie's cooperation in my Pray-for-Bikes project, I had to buy from him a 25-cent chance for the Knights of Columbus bazaar. That was bad enough. The worst was just below the headline, in slightly smaller type: "First Prize: Case of Scotch Whiskey."

There I was 11 years old, Dr. Qualben's son, indicted, convicted and about to be hung out to dry on three of Zion's felonies: gambling, messing with the Catholics (remember, this was 1946) and the booze business. Terrified, I tried to explain. Somehow my sentence was commuted to this: the K. of C. had to change my Cutty Sark first prize to a $50 U.S. Savings Bond (which they did).

A few days later, Dad drove me to the K. of C., where we picked up the bond, drove to the bank and cashed it in. Then we went to the bike shop where the bike was already set up. With my 80 cents in Burpee seed money plus the bond cash value, I rode out of there on my brand new blue Columbia bike!

Vinnie came running from his house yelling, "You got the bike!" "God answers prayer, Vinnie!" I yelled back. "When am I gonna get my red Schwinn, then?" he pestered, running alongside. "No way, Vinnie, you ain't gonna get it cuz you're a Kat-lik."

Those days were so different from how denominations see each other now. Zion Lutheran Church: I was born and raised there until I went to seminary. I never realized how much I learned from Zion until decades later. So much of this book's moorings were set deeply there, including how agreeing did not amount to a row of beans but *making symphony* meant so much more. Why? *So that* The Mission could get done!

How is it at your church? Are you spinning your wheels chasing after agreement or consensus rather than *making symphony* with each other...*so that* your Mission can happen?

Afterword

Faith illiteracy probably will increase as a problem in every denomination across the spectrum from millennialist to historically-rutted. That is, unless we re-examine *why* Christians study Scripture and doctrine.

Faith illiteracy precludes purposeful reliance on doctrine. Until our faith communities—from congregations through churchwide expressions—figure out why growth in Scripture and doctrine are important for *their* lives, church identity crises will cripple motivated support for individual members' maturity in these matters. In the meantime, corporate Christianity remains a tempting target for Bombsight Biblicism and other devices which demean the integrity of God's Word among us.

Purposeful Bible (and doctrine) study can be one way of getting at the motivational support problem. But it needs a participative focus (such as Christ-Care) if we are to unify individual and corporate motives for investing ourselves in faith literacy. With an operational focal point every Christian can claim, we will grow in how our doctrine *works* because we have linked our learning to a shared sense of *so that*...so that more important purposes can be accomplished!

3

Pathways for Conflict Redemption
Matthew 18:15-20

C onflict Redemption's normative *process* is summarized in a Bible passage which surrounds step-by-step procedure with a robust environment of promise and blessing. Along with "How-To" explanations comes an enriching progression of more important *so thats*, until the Great Promise verse. We are unaccustomed to seeing this text in such a light. Instead, we turn to this text in times of conflict and the Gospel is somehow filtered out.

Often these verses are referred to as the Church Discipline text, as Law. Why has it been kept in such bondage to the Law? Earlier scholars have not helped much. I believe that no other text in Scripture has been so abused for so long at such tragic loss to Christian relationships as has Matthew 18:15-20! Through these next chapters, I hope readers will come to a greater appreciation of these verses' magnificent treasury of blessing for the Body of Christ.

What we have in these six verses is *both* Law and Gospel. Which of these should predominate depends on the situation. For conflictors who clearly are among the wicked and impenitent and refuse to work in good faith with the other parties, then surgically precise application of the text's Law dimension is in order. Even then, it *always* must be exercised with a Gospel objective: to restore a conflictor to our relationship with him or her in the Body of Christ!

Its Gospel dimension prevails when conflictors participate in good faith and seek reconciliation for the sake of their *relationship,* rather than merely wishing to resolve the *issues.* Theirs are *redemptive* expectations as they seek ways and means to cope with problems *so that* their life together will be nourished and blessed by God.

Since every major doctrine in Scripture includes conflict, God's redemptive action and revelation usually happen in conflict contexts. In the midst of conflict between God and me, *in* Christ I am redeemed. As Christians we can expect redemption among conflicts in congregational life no less than in personal life!

What follows is a close examination of the pathways to Conflict Redemption, which are revealed and summarized in this jewel of a passage. The more one moves around this jewel, the more brilliant lights radiate from its facets. The text has not moved or changed. But as you return to it from now on, I hope new lights will shine from it into your life, and your life together.

These verses summarize and go far beyond a large body of rabbinic material. Whether or not they became Christians, even scholarly Jews who heard Jesus proclaim this text were awed by His mastery of the complex procedures. The more one studies those materials, the more impressive this brief passage's simple profundity becomes.

Since our opening comments may surprise you, we begin with an overview of this foundational passage for understanding the biblical Conflict Redemption *process.*

A Look at Matthew 18:15-20's Text

An informed translation of these verses can be a helpful start. This one honors the Greek text in the context of extensive first-century rabbinic usages which are only recently receiving long overdue careful study. (Italicized inserts are explanatory notes.)

Verse 15: **If your brother** (*another member of the church*) **trespasses** (*as in the Lords Prayer*) **against you, go and talk with him about his offense, between you and him alone** (*face-to-face*). **If he listens to you** (*i.e. if both of you do this in good faith*), **you will have been reconciled with your brother.**

Verse 16: **But if he does not respond to you, take one or two others with you so that every word may be confirmed in the presence of two or three fellow saints.** (***martyrwn,*** *the original word, here means "those who* **bear** *witness"*).

Verse 17a: **If you are not yet reconciled, inform the church** (*to get more help [resources, reinforcements, encouragement] for your joint efforts*).

Verse 17b: (*If your good faith efforts are still unsuccessful,*) **then bring it before the church** (*for adjudication; in our culture, may also involve litigation*). **If he refuses good faith, let him be under *menuddeh*** (*temporary demotion in church status, reserved for members such as "Gentiles and tax gatherers, mourners, sinners," etc.*).

Verse 18: **Truly I say to you, whatever you bind on earth shall have already been bound in heaven, and whatever you loose on earth shall have already been**

loosed in heaven. *(Grammatical note: the future perfect periphrastic with an aorist, used here, has basic doctrinal importance.)*

Verse 19: **Furthermore, I tell you that if two of you make symphony** *(symphoneisosin)* **in how you cope with your practical disputes** *(pragmatos, on earth),* **my father in heaven will bless your effort** *(literally: it will be ratified, its success guaranteed by Him).*

Verse 20: **Wherever two or three have been bound together** *(sunegnemoi, a passive participle; in this text the secondary sources stipulate: for Conflict Redemption!)* **in my name, I am present among them.**

GENERAL OBSERVATIONS

1. Context

One of the basic principles of responsible Bible study, *context,* locates the passage between two parables—the Lost Sheep and the Unmerciful Servant. The Lost Sheep theme of restoration is also the main objective of biblical Judaism's use of these procedures which Christ summarized. However, with the later parable, the objective is advanced beyond mere restoration to *reconciliation* within a religiously-based relationship.

A sheep wanders off. The shepherd leaves the "90-and-9" to find and bring back that *lost* sheep. (Note: it is lost; it is not bad. In Old Testament doctrine, *lost* is living under the Deceiver's handiwork.) It is quite clear that the next six verses are not about how to get rid of sheep, but how to reclaim and bring it back. The passage is not about how to exclude or excommunicate, but how to find and restore.

Later (vv. 21ff) Peter asks: How often do I have to go through this procedure toward Forgiveness? Seven times? He is asking Rabbi Jesus to affirm a criterion of "good faith" which prevailed at the time. With his "seventy-times-seven" response, Christ is telling Peter that it is a whole new "ball game," as it were. No longer merely an institutional matter (restoration), the procedure takes on some rather heavy *eternal* dimensions (*warning*, verse 35; *promise*, verses 19 and 20).

2. Text unit

All six verses comprise a closely-knit textual unit within the entire chapter's thematic development. Out of possible anti-Semitic ignorance, it used to be fashionable to chop this passage up into two separate "sayings," the first ending with verse 17b.

We now know that such a separation is textually indefensible, not only in terms of thematic development, but for technical reasons as well. For example, to cut off verses 18 through 20 from verse 17 would constitute an elementary violation of rabbinic law: No ban or curse has validity unless it is immediately followed by stipulation of a correlative blessing. Another example: the "two or three" of verse 20 refers back to those peace-builders in verses 15 and 16, as any religious Jew hearing Jesus knew full well.

UNDERLYING PRINCIPLES
OF MATTHEW 18:15-20

1. Personal Solution

Personal solution efforts are not only preferred but must be exhausted in good faith before conflictors can resort to having somebody else "solve" disruptive matters for them. Personal (or direct) solution means that those who have to live with the solution are better off creating it themselves. Why is this better?

a) The more complex the conflict, the more necessary it is for the conflictors to solve it. Only they know how to cut through all the complexities and get to essentials, to what they can not only live with but grow from, together.

b) If conflictors create the solution, it has a better chance of working and surviving. They have a vested ownership and interest in the solution's vitality.

c) If conflictors create the solution themselves, that fact encourages them to keep their *relationship* and personal reconciliation in proper priority over how they solve issues.

d) Strangely enough, conflictors already know the key ingredients of an eventual solution. However, typically those ingredients are bottled up by anger in the back of their heads. This may be why biblical [Ephesians 4:26, for example] and rabbinic procedures support the redemptive use of anger, if only to unlock those ingredients and get them on the table.

e) A basic principle of American jurisprudence is that personal solutions always take precedence over solutions created by courts, regulators or legislators, or adjudication—provided only that our solutions do not violate laws or legislative intent. Litigants come to agreement out of court and what happens? The judicial process stops, deferring to their personal solution.

2. Initiative

"He started it! So, he should make the first move."
"I am right and she is wrong. So, it is up to her to come
to me." From otherwise biblically literate Christians, we
often hear such tripe. But compare Matthew 18:15 with
Matthew 5:23.

In one text, the other person is at fault; in the Matthew 5 verse, *you* are at fault. In both texts, however,
what is our Lord's command? *You* go! Whoever is at
fault, *you* go! Christian, *you* take the initiative toward
solving the matter and moving toward reconciliation.
According to Scripture, a person who takes and sustains
good faith initiative toward reconciliation is marked as
a *Christian* in conflicted situations.

There is more than enough self-righteousness romp-
ing through conflicts without a congregation letting it
go unchecked. When another member gets up on his or
her ungodly high horse, it is our duty to help that
brother or sister in Christ dismount and to get on with
claiming this godly initiative for Conflict Redemption.

3. Redundancy

Redundancy means we have more than one opportunity and one way to work on conflict. Matthew 18:15-
20 is realistic in giving us this process for Conflict
Redemption. Because even our best efforts at one-on-
one (the First Step) may not be successful, there is more
support for your personal solution at the next Step, and
a more strongly supportive Step after that. Then comes
the recognition that if all personal solution Steps fail,
efforts at *indirect* solution may be called for.

On the other hand, the texts are quite clear that leap-
frogging to that failure Step (indirect solution) must
never be tolerated by a biblically faithful community.

4. Relationships

God-created and God-given relationships are the number one priority governing how Christians cope with their conflicts. Remember verse 19: "If two of you *make symphony* in how you settle any issue (*pragmatos*), God will bless your efforts." "What does our *relationship* need?" is far more important than whatever I think *I* need! Each of you probably has already wasted far too much time fantasizing over what *you* deserve, what you need, or what you are entitled to.

5. Immediacy

"Do not let the sun go down on your anger," lest you invite Satan to get his foot in the door on this matter. Do not wait until you are ready. That only complicates things, hardens the lines, and makes matters worse. Why? Because the "more suns go down on your anger" (Ephesians 4:25-26) the more *inflated* your sense of entitlement gets. Such little things are blown out of proportion by delay in taking the initiative, to put off going to that other person.

Delay pushes the situation and your relationship even higher into storm clouds. Like a lightning rod, your relationship starts getting "zapped" by long-building high voltage discharges from some otherwise unrelated storms.

6. The Whole Church Suffers

When there is a broken relationship among just two of its members, the whole church suffers. There is more to it than that well-known biblical exhortation to "bear one another's burdens." Scripture's stipulated mark of the True Church is the Bond of Peace (e.g. Ephesians 4:3) which is energized by the visible effects of God's love in Christ among us (e.g. Colossians 3:15 ff).

Yes, the Church is expected to be morally upright and faithful to apostolic teaching. Yet the Bond of Peace is singled out for such utmost priority. Why? God only knows, because we just can infer His reasons. My hunch is that without the Bond of Peace, we are disabled for getting the Job done.

YOM KIPPUR BACKGROUND

At the time of Christ, this emphasis on peace-builders' support by the Church was taken with utmost seriousness. Matthew 5:23ff is what biblical scholars term a homiletical gloss (expanded preaching) on the Liturgy for the Eve of Yom Kippur. That was the Day of Atonement, the Jews' Christmas-and-Easter rolled up into one ball of wax. Two fascinating provisions from standardized preparations for Yom Kippur illustrate the emphasis of this section.

a) If you are a peace-*breaker* in an everyday conflict, "God will not listen to any of your prayers," even on this Day of Atonement.

b) If stymied by a conflictor's bad faith peace-*breaking* attitude, a conflictor who has been exercising good faith in peace-*building* can rise before their congregation and declare suspension of the whole assembly's worship until God's people bring that peace-breaker into good faith participation in the process. This could even happen on the Day of Atonement!

This is powerful stuff, which underscores the utmost importance they placed on the believing community's supportive role in individual members' Conflict Redemption efforts.

However, I must underline a crucial point. These two items have only *informational* authority for us. For Christians, they do not have *revelatory* or biblical authority! (I mention this lest some misguided soul stirs up a ruckus at your next Easter service by trying to invoke these informational items.) Nonetheless, it reminds us how seriously our biblical predecessors took this point: the whole church has a direct stake in supporting individual members' need to cope with disruptive problems through the Conflict Redemption process.

Throughout Scripture, the other face on the Do-the-Right-Thing coin shows Christians traveling these Do-It-Right pathways which lead to new life and vitality in our God-created relationships!

HOW MANY STEPS ARE THERE?

The number of Steps we discern in Matthew 18:15-20 depends on conflictors' sincere attitudes. Are their attitudes toward the conflict *redemptive?* Or are they proceeding in bad faith with a corrupt attitude? (The Lutheran Confessions, for example, refer to this latter category as "the wicked and impenitent.")

With peace-*breakers* operating in bad faith, there are *three* Steps. Why? To bring them to their senses through corporate imposition of the Law, so that they will re-enter the process in good faith. Those three Steps follow juridical models and have been well known under the rubric of Church Discipline.

If the first two Steps failed, the believing community (in the ancient unitary coalescence of what we now call Church-and-State) ended up deciding the case through a *Bet Din* (church court) procedure.

But there are *Five* Steps for peace-*building* conflictors who would proceed in good faith with a redemptive attitude and expectation. Since various denominational traditions have included disciplinary applications of this text in their catechectical instruction and customs for many years, we will concentrate on the text's *redemptive* purpose in the following sections: the Five Steps of Matthew 18:15-20.

Matthew 18's Five Step Process for Conflict Redemption

Step One: **One-on-One, face-to-face meeting between you and the other conflictor, alone.**

FIRST MEETINGS

Because most of us are nervous about going one-on-one with the other "party," we are tempted to "stack the deck" in our favor or worry whether the other person has done so. Indeed, this understandable uneasiness may be a major reason why so many Christians hopscotch through Matthew 18. "Let's get the issues out in the open and talk about them" is a common slogan among biblical illiterates and Christian cowards. A few suggestions from practical experience with this text may be helpful.

Initiative—Christ's clear command is that *you* take and sustain initiative for getting reconciliation underway. If the other person reciprocates or even beats you to it, thank God! Do not delay. "That is too soon," or, "I need time to prepare," are excuses that will only make matters more difficult. A helpful response might be, "I am not prepared either, but I want us to start straightening things out." Do not even speculate about who is at fault *or* what that other person has done to you.

Setting for the Meetings—Try to meet in a place such as your church sanctuary. In doing so, you are recovering an ancient tradition which modern propriety has foolishly forsaken. Once together, argue and be angry if need be. Yes, even in full view of God's altar. God's people have done it that way for centuries. *Why* in church? Because those surroundings will keep supporting your desire to work out the situation *redemptively.* Ample research has shown that the setting heavily shapes our expectations. If your distressed relationship is with a pastor, for example, never have this one-on-one meeting in the pastor's office. It puts that pastor in a *power* position.

Duration of Meetings—Agree to set aside *at least* two hours apiece for your first sessions, especially when one or both of you feel strongly about the conflict. Why that long? More often than not, conflictors need at least that much time to exchange speeches. Before both of you can move on to sorting things out and working through them, each must have the opportunity to get things off his or her chest. Only then can you get on with seeing and building upon God's Peace.

Focus of Meetings—It is human nature for us to want to emphasize *my* needs and *my* rights. The meeting's focus should be on what is happening to your *relationship* within the Body of Christ, and to your various "One New Person" relationships. However, when you start zeroing in on your relationship, *do not focus on more than one of these relationships at any session.* Otherwise, you will overload the process. Consider together how other relationships may influence the situation. But keep your *focus* clear.

Discretion—"Between you and him (her) alone" means just that. Both of you must commit to keeping all communication regarding the conflict limited to the two of you. If others are supporting your mutual effort, they are to know only two things: (1) that both of you are meeting in good faith, and when (2) you have been reconciled with each other.

Sequence—Make sure that those involved are familiar with Conflict Redemption's purposes and process. Otherwise one or more of you may enter into the process with conflicting goals or agendas. Another informed Christian may help by reviewing some of the key principles of this process with all of you before you begin your work.

1. Prayer

Begin with a brief prayer by each participant. Themes might include: "We ask you to bind us together into this process in your Name. Open our eyes to see more clearly again that relationship you created for us....Grant to each of us the gifts of discernment, wisdom and grace so that we may delight in our bond as One New Person in Christ, and so that our work together will nourish and strengthen that bond...."

Conclude your beginning with this doxology: "Glory be to the Father, and to the Son, and to the Holy Spirit. As it was in the beginning, is now, and ever shall be, world without end. Amen."

2. Mutual Inquiry

Then ask each other: *"When did our situation get really troublesome for you?"* As you talk, one or both of you may begin to recall even earlier "connections" you had almost forgotten.

"What else was going on in your (or our) life about that time?"

At first glance, it might seem there are no connections. Often, this question will not connect until later on. Why not? Because we tend to have one-track minds and tunnel vision in conflicts. We think our trouble is a case of one straw that broke an injured camel's back. So, do you rescue the camel, or keep bickering over getting your fair share of that straw?

More often the situation is like a lighted match thrown into an already volatile gas tank. Something probably happened that caused one or both of you to explode. The explosion then inflamed distresses already present in your One New Person relationship.

Deflections from personal distress onto church conflict may become apparent. It is necessary to broaden your outlook for other trouble generators because Body of Christ relationships in a congregation also can get short-circuited from outside sources. *"When did things get really bad here at Bethany?"* Ask six members and there will probably be six different times identified. These times often coincide with *other* distresses going on in that member's life. When somebody's church or home One New Persons (see page 35) do not come through, he or she may become understandably angry and *over-react* to any issue that comes along. This brief digression illustrates a need to be alert for influences whose impact on your personal situation might not have dawned on you before.

3. Mutual history

"Let us sort out what has been going on, so that we can agree on what came after what." Not: Who was at fault? But: What has *happened?* You may disagree on the "what was said" parts of this history, especially if too

many suns have gone down on the situation. Construct a mutual history of what has actually happened.

Even at this stage of your discussion, see if both of you can venture into: "What I *should* have said is...." Be advised that this history-making probably will revolve around your ego's, on what you feel it did to *each* of you.

"What happened that undermined our relationship?"

Then reconstruct your trouble's mutual history around this more important relationship perspective. When you have moved into this process, try to channel any expressed anger toward what has been done to your *relationship*. *Do* express anger! You have Scriptural warrant for doing so, but *not* for a fault-finding or self-righteous anger!

If necessary, be angry at the other(s). Even detail your feelings and get them on the table. But keep trying to channel each other's anger toward the *real* victim in all this: your relationship!

"I know what I need."

More likely, it is what you *want* rather than what you *need*. Exchanging Wish Lists does not help much. Rather, ask each other the following two questions—go on to the second one when both of you are finished with the first:

a) "What do *you* need to have happen for things to turn around for us in this situation?" *Not:* "What do I have to do to satisfy you?"

b) "What does our *relationship* need? What needs to happen so we can be reconciled and back on track, even though we may never see eye-to-eye on all things?"

4. Agenda Setting

Before your next session, who does: What? How?

When?   Given Christ's seventy-times-seven response to Peter (verse 21), do not be surprised if the
major outcome from your first session or two is
agreeing to meet again. Do not depart this meeting
without making a specific appointment for your
next session! Schedule it for as soon as possible;
otherwise, whatever progress you both have made
will deteriorate rapidly.

If you both feel there is still a lot more to sort out:

a) Consider the other's response to those two Needs
   questions. In thinking them over, are there some
   changes due in how *you* first responded to those
   questions? Do not waste time on how valid the
   other's responses were, or you will yank the whole
   process back to square one. That is an ego trip.
b) Retrace that mutual history the two of you developed, in light of both sets of Needs responses.
   Before you meet again: Are there some key items in
   that history which do not seem all that "key" *now*?
c) Are possibilities occurring to you about useful ways,
   steps or resources which could help deal with troubles in his or her *other* relationships? Troubles which
   surfaced in this previous session?

    If your one-on-one session moves closer to a "Peace
Agreement," write down its key features before concluding the session:

a) *Agreement in Principle* is your mutual agreement
   about what has to happen to solve specific disrup-
   tions in your God-given relationship. It need not be
   a detailed solution to your disagreements. Rather,
   it should be regarded as the foundation upon which
   both of you will work on those disagreements.

b) *Responsibilities* for implementing your agreement: who does what, when, how? Be specific on the follow-up step(s) you agreed to, perhaps in a one-step-at-a-time scenario.

Immediately upon writing down these specific features of your Peace-Agreement, go together to your church's altar with your handwritten Agreement. Do not put off doing this!

5. *Presentation of your Peace-Agreement*

Both or all parties place this Agreement on the Altar (or large Bible), each one briefly lifting and replacing it. Then, go to the rail to kneel, facing the altar. Each one of you may begin the first part of this brief Presentation.

Both: *In the Name of the Father, and of the Son, and of the Holy Spirit. Amen.*

One: *Heavenly Father, you have promised that if we bring our burdens to Christ, our Prince of Peace, you will bless our work throughout eternity when we try to make symphony with each other about these things. Bless me and (name the other[s]) as we continue this work.*

Other: *Lord, we have come to a Peace-Agreement about matters which have come between us and, together, we have placed it upon your Altar for your Blessing. Encourage us and renew our bond with our One New Person in Christ from now on.*

Both: *Bless us, Father, and make us a blessing. Our Father, who art in heaven, hallowed be Thy Name.....*

Rise (to Share the Peace of Christ): *The Peace of Christ be with you, my* (brother / sister) *in Christ.*
Go forth in God's Bond of Peace!

Beware

Beware of statements such as these during your use of this First Step:

"It is hopeless."

One practical corollary of the biblical doctrine of Righteousness is that Satan is the Deceiver who can suffocate a "righteous new creation" relationship under his layers of deception. That relationship is "hopeless" only if none of us care to peel away each layer, or one of us deliberately wants that relationship to *die*. (Does "hopeless" signal the fact you have some yum-yum waiting in the closet?) Some of us do lack skills for removing those layers of deception under which the relationship may have been lost. Nonetheless, while Scripture does recognize that a One New Person relationship may die, *it had better not be the victim of murder!* This has to be one of the basic reasons for Matthew 18.

"We could straighten this out if you would go for counseling."

This is one of the oldest ploys for avoiding one's own responsibilities in a situation and for erecting a barricade against listening to another person. *"Both of us could benefit from counseling"* is an altogether different matter.

However, in terms of Matthew 18:15-20, professional help belongs to Step Three. While it can be useful or necessary, none of you must allow the possibility of seeking such additional help to subvert your personal responsibility and your good faith efforts in this *First* Step.

"I am not over-reacting!"

Over-reaction to a comment or issue mandate a *re-*

sponse rather than an equal reaction. As a general rule: over-reactions signal that a more significant matter is surging toward the surface. "What is *really* wrong?" is one helpful response, provided it is sincere and provided you are patient. But do move on if the logjam beneath that over-reaction will not break up. (Lacking the expertise, none of us should ever attempt to play psychiatrist or psychologist!)

"I am Right! I know I am Right on this!"

Even mature Christians will be tempted to twist Matthew 18's Conflict Redemption process into a juridical atmosphere or procedure. "That is not what this is all about," is an appropriate response. "We are searching for what we really need out of all this, and for what we can start doing about it."

Who is right, who is wrong, or who is the guilty party amounts to a black hole in spiritual space, which will devour whatever is left of your relationship. For any faithful Christian, doing the Right thing takes precedence over being Right. It cannot be Right if that thing kills a "righteous new creation" relationship, can it?

"I have something to say."

Too often, your first session goes nowhere because one or both of you come into it repeating set speeches. This is one reason for allowing at least two hours for a Step One session. This will allow time to verbalize such statements so both of you can proceed on God's pathways to reconciliation. Saying what is on your mind is an important privilege. If you prevent it, you undermine the process and Step One collapses into a dialogue of the deaf.

However, once the other(s) start *repeating* themselves, two things should happen:

a) "You have already said that today." (*Not:* "We have already been over that" [a thousand times] because, in reality, you have *not* been over it already *within this process.*)

b) Realize that the repetition signals probable readiness to move on to subsequent steps.

Afterword

Conflict has a habit of filtering out the Gospel, a reason why Matthew 18 has been kept in bondage to the Law ("Church Discipline"). Centuries of neglect by biblical scholarship has deprived us of this text's profound theology, evangelical practicality and powerful promises. Rediscovery of rabbinic principles and procedures only emphasizes the mastery and distinctive Christ-centeredness of verses 15-20 in this landmark chapter in Matthew's gospel.

Walking pathways to true forgiveness, reconciliation and vitality in one or more of our God-created relationships: that is the major purpose of this passage. Putting legs on textual themes which enable us to move confidently within Matthew 18's letter and spirit requires familiarity with Talmudic and earlier sources most of us have not yet studied. So, I have combined insights from such sources with parish realities to help Christians accomplish this passage's purposes.

4

Seventy Times Seven

I f, after several Step One sessions, it is conflictors' mutual sense that they could use some help sorting through their situation or to get over some brick walls, it is appropriate for conflictors to be joined by one or two Fellow Saints. We have had to coin a new word to identify their qualifications and functions, since there is no equivalent modern term for this distinctively biblical role.

The usage history of *martyrwn* / Fellow Saints simply does not permit assumptions that the original term equals today's "mediator" or "arbitrator" in either conflict resolution or juridical contexts. While mediation can be a blessing, to equate its judicial character with Step Two in the Bible's redemptive process is to mix apples with oranges.

Step Two: Use of Audicators

Audi-cator: This new word is a combination of *audio* (I listen or hear what is to be heard; e.g. Matthew 11:15) and *authenticator*.

Audicators are the *martyrwn* (martyrs: those who *bear* witness) of Matthew 18:16. When we consider Paul's reference to them in Galatians 6 and I Corinthians 6, rabbinic scholars will recognize a well-established precedent for this early church practice. They were the "Righteous Ones" or "more Spiritual among you" (the *tzaddikim*, in late Old Testament practice). Their role in personal or corporate use of the Conflict Redemption process is to help conflictors experience *redemptive* outcomes from conflict.

Conflictors ask these Fellow Saints to sit in with them to help them see beneath surfaces to discern what *God* is accomplishing and has already accomplished in their situation, and to help them focus on real needs.

Seeing God's Purposes in Ordinary Life

According to Luke 2:25-35, Simeon (in the Temple) was such a Righteous One. For years Simeon witnessed ordinary Presentations scenes. Then one day, he suddenly erupts with his *(nunc dimittis)*: "Now let your servant depart in peace. For my eyes have now *seen* your salvation!" To other eyes, Mary and Joseph and the Babe were just another ordinary new family honoring an old custom. But not to this Righteous One, Simeon! His *eyes* saw beneath the surface of things to what was really going on here!

For the Righteous One Christian, the whole landscape of life looks Christian because he or she sees what God is accomplishing in, with or under ordinary things—even your conflict. This Righteous One does *not* judge who is right, does not mediate, counsel or tell parties what to do. The Righteous One is a revealer who helps you peel away each layer which confuses or blinds you within your One New Person relationships. Christian, that is after all where it all *really* began for you.

The Audicator *hears* in order to help conflictors discern what is really happening, *and* call to their attention the eventual solution's ingredients, which the conflictors themselves usually reveal without realizing they have done so.

This distinctive revelatory function requires qualities which not all Christians may have in full enough measure. This is why Audicators were always selected by the church rather than self-appointed. The same should be true today.

Conflictors themselves may choose their Audicators from among a larger number which the church has chosen and authorized for this role. In Scripture and today, Audicators include men and women, laity as well as the ordained. Theirs is not an authoritative function, nor has it ever been designated as a specific Office in the church. It is a biblically-mandated function by Fellow Saints who have been called to other vocations or offices.

Audicator's Three-Fold Authentication Role

1. **Authenticate the support and encouragement of the whole Body of Christ for these peace-builders;**

2. **Authenticate their good faith, in the event recourse to later Steps in the process may be indicated or necessary.**

   One of several Audication tests for conflictors' good faith revolves around two ancient questions (ascribed to Paul's teacher, Gamaliel and/or his approximate contemporary, Akiba):

   "Tell me what his (or her) real needs are."

   Ask each conflictor this question in the other's presence. Expect interruptions because a major purpose of this inquiry is to cut down to realistic size the other conflictor's usually inflated sense of entitlement. By engaging each conflictor in this question, the process also expands their usually *deflated* or underestimated sense of limits for making concessions.

"Tell me what your relationship's real needs are."

This second question helps move conflictors to the heart of the matter, to where essential improvements are most needed and possible. Since the best route around ego barricades is to go *over* them, this question helps conflictors do just that.

3. **Authenticate their need for more help from or through the Church.**

This is done if, in the Audicators' opinion, specific further help is necessary. Prior to moving from the First Step to use of an Audicator, conflictors agree that this decision has to be the Audicator's. Why? Because we are so easily tempted to give up and to get somebody else to fix things, to bail out and flee to later Steps. A conflictor should expect to have others closely scrutinize his or her real motives whenever that party backs off with: "I cannot do it."

Two Types of Audication

Informal **Audication**—This agenda presumes that conflictors will be able to create a solution back at Step One. They meet with an Audicator(s) to enhance and encourage their best efforts to eventually work it out one-on-one. Moving back and forth between these first two Steps is common and often advisable, given our frequent lack of confidence and courage in direct reconciliation.

Intensive **Audication**—Intensive Audication seeks creation of a Peace-Agreement at Step (Two). Conflictors proceed with this agenda when it becomes apparent that further progress, one-on-one, is unlikely without having a Peace-Agreement foundation in place.

Typically, a lot of complications and failed solution attempts precede recourse to Intensive Audication. Two Intensive Audications in which I participated were preceded by failed attempts at courts' intervention, for example, with lawsuits filed, well-meant "mediation" debacles, juridical arbitration, and pastors' counseling. There were two crucial reasons for the success of these sessions: (1) The problems were so complex that only the conflictors themselves could work it out; and (2) these conflictors were Christians who craved a redemptive outcome.

Intensive Audications are lengthy events. A five to six hour non-stop session is common. Procedures used have become clearly patterned, while leaving plenty of leeway for adjustments and adaptation. Obviously, some training in procedure and hands-on experience is advisable for Audicators who are willing to participate in Intensive Audication.

Audicator Training

Training of Audicators always occurs through the initiative and auspices of regional church jurisdictions. A change in this basic policy is not anticipated, given the biblical qualification and selection principles for Audicators. Audicators function within the polity of your denomination, not as another program but as a direct service to congregations. (Note suggestions on training in Chapter 14.)

In the event that personal solution efforts are not successful, and these first Three Steps have to be recast in a juridical mode (in light of the matter coming to Step Four), no one should think this change cancels the text's *redemptive* objective and character. In such cases, Audicators' roles are limited to: (1) authenticating good faith use of the prior Steps, and (2) helping with any possibilities for "regressing" portions of all of the dispute back into earlier Steps. Those possibilities materialize more often than one might imagine. It can be an enormous encouragement to the parties to have Audicators' help available to support their willingness to try again.

Audicators are a uniquely biblical resource for God's People. Welcome back among us, Righteous Ones!

Step Three: More Help from Church

Only within the last generation have Christian denominations intentionally worked to equip congregations' mutual ministries with expertise for members' psycho-emotional and relationship difficulties.

Not so long ago, a common attitude prevailed: if you are having such trouble, it must be a sure sign of either God's judgment upon you, or that the Holy Spirit has departed from your life and vocation. This attitude was also shared by many of the ordained. Thank God, we have come to our senses!

Most seminaries provide training and hands-on experience in counseling for marital, family and personal problems. As yet, far too few equip their students for help in members' alcoholism and other abuse troubles. Fortunately, church-affiliated hospitals, clinics and counseling centers have established resources which pastors and congregations can call upon for expert and intensive help. After a generation of mass higher education and television, church members today are much more knowledgeable about these things, including these resources' limits.

While there is no such thing as *Christian* psychiatry any more than there is Christian economics, there is an ample resource of heartfelt Christians doing psychiatry, sociology, psychology and counseling. Whether in private practice or employed by church institutions, their number is substantial and increasing. They are available to help us when needed.

In terms of Matthew 18:15-20, *professional* assistance is but one form of more help from the church, however. The first half of verse 17, "inform the Church," has extensive expressions throughout both Old and New Testament experience. The concept of the congregation as a *helping* people who provide for others in time of need was well established and expected. Financial assistance for outside help could be forthcoming, as well as personal and corporate reinforcements of the Conflict Redemption process.

Typified by provisions for *Yom Kippur,* we noted earlier the Apostolic church's sense of corporate responsibility for members who are reconciling disrupted relationships. This supplements those oft-repeated variations on a theme of bearing one another's burdens.

On the other hand, for the peace-*breaker* this helping aspect of "informing the church" is governed by our corporate use of the Law so long as that member continues in impenitent bad faith. However, in Step Three we cannot assume that help from the church is altogether prohibited to such impenitent persons. We recognize that until help for a conflictor's possible addiction or mental illness is forthcoming, for example, this person remains bogged down in the Law. He or she may not come to their senses without experiencing how the power of the Gospel is at work in the fellowship which their behavior has scorned.

In working with congregations, Audicators usually are perceived as being called in at Step Three (More Help from the Church) but, as they continue Audication with a congregation, their role increasingly enhances the process's first two Steps.

Forms of More Help from the Church

The Conflict Redemption process of Matthew 18:15-20 clearly precludes jumping to this Third Step without good faith use of Steps One or Two! More help may be used concurrently with these primary Steps, as a supplementary aid. But it must not be used to displace them, as an avoidance mechanism. Any assistance must merely supplement the text's *personal solution* emphasis. There are at least three forms of help from the church.

- **Professional Expertise**
- **Encouragement from the Church**
- **Christ-Care Commitments**

Professional expertise—Professional expertise is not only in order for mental illness, severe relational distresses, addictions, adulthood impacts from childhood sexual or physical abuse, but also for help with working out difficulties over a chaotic family system or relationship. Other forms of expertise may be indicated, such as fiscal, legal or managerial specialists.

Encouragement from the church—Various practical and innovative forms of encouragement from the Body of Christ should not be underestimated. Where should the focus be? Conflict often involves plenty of suffering. Loneliness is one of its toughest components. With so much emotional drain going on, energy for perseverance is in short supply; but it can gain nourishment from the Body.

If a congregation addresses its forms of encouragement to (1) diminish conflictors' isolation or sense of going it alone, and (2) reinforce their persistence in the sometimes lengthy process of building upon God's gift of peace in Christ, you have made an important and appreciated contribution to those conflictors' efforts. Here are a couple of examples.

Peace-building banners

Several congregations have a free-standing peace-building (or Reconciled by Christ) banner in or near the chancel. Each time members have experienced God's blessing in use of Conflict Redemption, a long ribbon or other symbol is added to the center pole. This encourages others and is a reminder to those reconciled.

If appropriate, announcement is made prior to adding another ribbon, usually with no detail. Names are mentioned only with the parties' prior approval. If their previous difficulties were known in the congregation, it is important that their success in reconciliation also be recognized and cherished.

Centuries ago, it was customary for peace-builders to bring a joint gift in thanksgiving. The banner additions can be an encouraging symbolic gift within that old tradition.

Prayer support

Prayer support is powerful encouragement to conflictors. Be sure they know it is occurring. Use common sense safeguards lest the congregation's procedures for enlisting prayer support deteriorate from a Body of Christ expression to a kind of voyeurism by *busybodies* of Christ.

Christ-Care commitments and resources

The term Christ-Care means "doing unto others as Christ would do unto you." Christ-Care means embodying the same compassionate love in Christ with each other that we have known in Christ personally. We treat persons and relationships the same way Christ treats us. Christ-Care begins with those closest to us, or personally known. Christ-care extends from that personal experience to our congregation. Which, in turn, reinforces our Christ-care within Monday's world.

This is an over-simplified summary of an effective heritage for which we have written an extensive Bible Study. Here, Christ-care congregations are urged to provide purposeful support to peace-builders throughout their use of Conflict Redemption.

Give no thought to whom you think may be at fault or is the innocent party! Remember: Christ told us to "visit me when I was in prison." Certifiably a *guilty* party! Try to focus the church's Christ-caregiving not only on their most obviously troubled relationship but also on their other One New Person relationships. For example, focus support on their family US while they strive for healing in marriage.

When conflictors experience how their congregation supports personal use of the Conflict Redemption process, their prospects for success are enhanced. An extraordinary watershed for their personal growth in Christ has been replenished.

Step Four: Third Party Solution

"Inform the church" that good faith use of all prior Steps has been exhausted without success. The conflictors have been unable to create a solution themselves, despite everyone's hard work, persistence and best efforts. It happens and not always because of evil conspiracies, either! A third party or entity has to create a solution for these conflictors.

FORMATS FOR STEP FOUR

Call in regional church jurisdictions

For a congregation, this Step usually takes the form of calling in a regional church officer or staff, court of adjudication or another established intervention procedure for making a judgment.

An ad hoc delegation might go to the regional office to complain about trouble in their congregation. If that judicatory office has selected and trained Audicators and other resources for Matthew 18's Conflict Redemption process, it becomes possible to begin *regressing* the situation back through previous Steps.

Please note: Where immorality or scandalous life, false doctrine, offensive conduct or other ordination-violating offenses have clearly occurred, timely disciplinary action by the regional judicatory must run its course.

Use of the Conflict Redemption process in such situations may be focused more appropriately upon the impacts created by these offenses. Typical impacts needing to be dealt with include corporate as well as personal hurts, angers, demoralization, confusion, dysfunction and loss of direction.

Bring it before your church council, board or congregational meeting.

With few exceptions, this move usually violates Matthew 18:15-20. Unless it can be verified that all three previous Steps have been exhausted in good faith, the Chair *must* rule:

1. this overture is out of order,
2. specify its reference back to Step Three (Two, or One), and
3. suggest specific Conflict-Redemption assistance for the ones who have "brought up" the matter.

Regardless of Robert's Rules and Parliamentary Procedure, any overture at a public forum in the church which bypasses the previous Steps of Matthew 18:15-20 must be ruled out-of-order, without discussion or voting permitted. Unless, of course, the congregation wishes to throw out the primary Articles of its Constitution. Robert's Rules are cited in a Bylaw; wherever they contradict a clear procedural stipulation in Scripture, Robert's Rules must be overruled. No Bylaw can supercede a primary Article of your Constitution!

Congregations are losing expensive lawsuits for ignoring the spirit, authority and letter of Matthew 18:15-20!

Go to court

A husband and wife file for divorce. They have exhausted the previous steps. Audicators verify they have proceeded in good faith. That is the only report these Audicators should provide, with extreme exceptions and subject only to laws governing confidentiality. This form of Step Four also includes possible arbitration or using other specialists, *within* the text's purposes.

In case you have not noticed: from sea to shining sea America is hauling itself off to court. We have become the most litigious society in history. Churches at all levels of expression, including the typical denomination and its affiliated congregations and judicatories, are facing hundreds of millions of dollars in lawsuits brought by their own members.

If there are foot-draggers in your midst who do not yet resonate to the positive blessing of congregational support for members' reliance on Conflict Redemption, they may well be reminded of the alternative's costly consequences.

Gossip and public accusation

If I present or pass along accusations which turn out to be false, misleading or only partially true, Scripture regards my action as a case of Murder. Remember the case of Mordecai and Haman? Haman (Esther 7) goes to the gallows for the crime he had tried to pin on Mordecai. The gossiper or accuser gets the penalty due the crime of which another is falsely accused. For example, if I falsely accused someone of adultery, I would be stoned to death. Capital offense gossip was the kind that murdered a One New Person (marriage, family, neighbor, citizen, vocation, church or my *In* Christ "US"). So also, the early church could not decide which was worse: heretic or schismatic, because both of them would kill the Body of Christ.

"But this is a *public matter*, so Matthew 18:15-20 does not apply," some would say. There is a paragraph in Luther's *Large Catechism* (#284, on Bearing False Witness) which has been invoked to justify publication of attacks on fellow members of a denomination, *without* first exhausting good faith use of Matthew 18. There are three problems with this "public matter" excuse:

1. **Historical Contrast**—The last mainstream reformer to go one-on-one with the Pope was Jan Hus, who was executed forthwith. Luther resorted to the printing press. But how many of today's media adversaries in your church risk being burned at the stake?

2. **Out of Context** use of #284. Luther's emphasis in this section (about not bearing false witness) was on *reconciliation* and upon putting "the best construction" on what we hear about our neighbor. "Defend him against the poisonous tongues of those who pry out and pounce on something to criticize in their neighbor, misconstruing and twisting things in the worst way. This is what happens now especially to the precious Word of God and its preachers" (#289).

3. **Public Insult to the final authority of God's Word.** People are not fools when it comes to discerning what authority actually governs media adversaries. Several denominations have been wracked by, and possibly self-destructing over, controversies which provide blunt testimony to the tragic costs from ignoring good faith recourse to Matthew 18's Conflict Redemption process.

Step Four: A Tragic Necessity

Going to Step Four is tragic because at best this is a battlefield tourniquet applied to stem the bloodletting. More often, it amounts to a funeral over a One New Person relationship which, to all intents and purposes, has died.

Personal Solution Must Be the Standard

In Labor-Management relations, this step is regarded as a failure for collective bargaining. In any healthy society, recourse to the indirect solutions of Step Four signals a breakdown of the norm: Personal Solution must be the standard.

In both Old and New Testaments, bringing your conflict into juridical disposition is permitted only when good faith use of all Personal Solution procedures has been exhausted. Jumping over the other Steps to Step Four is more than an insult to the Church. Scripture regards this as a denial of the Body (e.g. I Corinthians 6:1-9a; Galatians 6:1-5; cf. the scenario in Matthew 5:23 ff). Surely, it is scandalous for any Christian church to elect or honor leaders who are litigation addicts in their everyday lives while posturing as pious Pharisees around the church.

Excommunication

"Let him be unto you as a Gentile or Tax Collector" (verse 17b) is usually seen as a mandate for excommunication or exclusion. While there are mandates for excommunication elsewhere in the New Testament, such a mandate is *not* in Matthew 18.

Technically, what we have in Matthew 18:17b is a rabbinic *menuddeh*. That is, a demotion in status which was imposed on "gentiles, Jews, publicans, mourners, widows" and the like. It usually was a temporary, though renewable, demotion for 30 to 45 days.

For example, in Christ's parable of the Pharisee and Publican Praying, the Publican was not *outside* the church but inside, at a "place in the back." This is why Jesus could socialize and fellowship with Matthew, Zacchaeus and various low lifes: they were under *menuddeh* (or possibly, the less severe *niddui* and/or *nezifah*). If they had been excommunicated (*herem*), his association with them would have devastated his teaching authority.

The formula for *herem*--actual "cutting off from the Body"—is not present in this text. While there are sound textual bases for this practice in other passages, there is a much larger problem with how churches today use excommunication or exclusion procedures. (See Mark 9:43-47; I Corinthians 5:1-13, 12:26; compare Chapter 5 with II Corinthians 2:5-12, if Paul is referring to the same person.)

The major problem comes when those exclusion procedures ignore the emphatic biblical and confessional objective of bringing back the lost sheep, of reconciliation with the conflictor(s). The strategic purpose of *menuddeh* resembles modern sanctions, such as the secular Strike or Lock-Out. Sanctions are invoked in order to pressure the other party into good faith participation in the negotiating process. So also with *menuddeh:*
1. To pressure the conflictor(s) to participate in good faith in the Conflict Redemption process, so that
2. Reconciliation will be accomplished.

Therefore, before sending out letters or notices to inactives or moving to drop them from the rolls, clear biblical principles should be honored:

1. Has our Board or Council geared up and committed itself to the diligent work of *regaining* these brothers and sisters? If not, will sending out those letters constitute a serious abrogation of our corporate responsibility?

2. Have we found out whether they are *burned* wood rather than *dead* wood? Perhaps there was a failure in our shared ministries to them in times of personal crisis which may have triggered their dropping out. If such was the occasion, the church further alienates them if you are just asking them to come back to church, because that is a low-level response to high-level crisis. At a minimum, begin with: "How can we help?"

3. If you discover that barriers are too high between them and your congregation, make a concerted effort to see they enter into another congregation's life and ministry. Many drop outs and dissidents join other congregations without encouragement from you, of course.

    A suggestion: The next time you have a *Congregational Bond of Peace Service* [sample in Chapter 15], take the time and effort to personally invite these ex-members to participate in this service with you. "We are not trying to trick you into coming back. We want your membership in your new congregation to be even more of a blessing to you and to others, without being burdened by hurts and disappointments you experienced here. This service is an occasion when all of us can let go of the past in a way which gives us a godly foundation for healing and renewal to happen."

Old hurts brought into their new congregation often turn such members into *poison pills* in that Body. Whether privately or through its annual *Bond of Peace Service*, a receiving congregation is advised to do intentional biblical ministry to those hurts and angers, whether or not the previous congregation has done so.

4. Are we proceeding in a manner which neither forecloses nor cripples the possibility of reconciliation with these lost sheep from our fold? Are we telling ourselves something about our motives and priorities when we keep calling them dead wood, inactives or drop-outs, rather than lost sheep?

If Indirect Solution Actions Become Necessary—If the congregation chooses to call in somebody from your regional church jurisdiction to decide matters, here are some suggestions.

1. **Receive that person(s) in a *pastoral* role,** rather than automatically throw this work into a Judgment tunnel. "Can you help us deal with this situation?" *Not:* "Just tell us, is the Pastor going to stay or leave?" *Or,* "Who is right?"

2. **Decision delivery**—If a difficult and tough decision has to be rendered, the congregation's corporate life will suffer for years afterwards if you avoid taking a firmly redemptive posture toward how that decision is going to be delivered and carried out.

3. **Steps regression**—While the overall situation has mandated your need for an Indirect Solution, are there loose ends in the mix of things which may need

attention at prior steps in the Conflict Redemption process? *For example,* are there individuals who should work on peace-breaking problems between or among themselves? If so, who sees to this?

The more intense a conflicted situation and the longer it has gone on, the more complicated it will seem to be. While a portion of your congregation may be tempted to throw in the towel and resort to an Indirect Solution course of action, there may be better possibilities for sorting things out and setting practical agendas for dealing with the situation. That is, if there is a pervasive desire for the congregation to do better, to move toward vitality from what has been going on. With that expectation, you may be able to move back to Step Three: more help from or through the larger church.

Indeed, do not be surprised if you move into Step Four and discover that most, if not all, of your troubles can be worked out through the prior Steps. Be open to that possibility. The integrity and vitality of your congregation are far better served by creating a blessed solution at one or more of those earlier Steps!

Churchwide Step Four Systems

Secular courts are encouraging "litigation alternatives" to court trials or hearings: private mediation, binding arbitration and other forms of directive help for dispute resolution when the parties have been unable to create their own solution. Not only does this development ease clogged court dockets but, more basically, it improves chances for equitable and durable solutions and restores responsibility for creating solutions to those who have to live with them.

Nationwide denominations are also moving to create "adjudication alternatives" for situations where members' own efforts at reconciliation and dispute resolution have not been successful. Earlier, the next step would be Adjudication, bringing the matter to a kind of latter-day *Bet Din* or church court jurisdiction and procedure. For all intents and purposes, however, this step was so litigatory in tone and manner that the sole major difference from secular courts usually was the auspices. Rarely has this process worked well. As an expression of our basic beliefs in action, the process was bound to fail.

The Lutheran Church-Missouri Synod, for example, has moved beyond repairing outmoded machinery and toward a new philosophy and procedure for Step Four. Not only belief-ful and purposeful, such a dispute resolution system should work much better than the old Adjudication process which they and other denominations have used. If your denomination is considering similar improvements in how Step Four is handled, I can offer several suggestions.

1. Watch your language! Avoid terminology associated with litigation, regardless of how you might try to redefine it. What people hear is more decisive than whatever you mean. *Mediator* and *mediation* are two overused terms which will undermine members' perception of your new procedure's purposes and character. (Others have suggested the term *reconciliator* which, I think, is much more appropriate to a biblical spirit and usage.)

2. Reconciliation is the desired outcome, above and beyond case resolution. Whatever procedures you develop should enhance prospects for achieving that greater--and biblical--purpose.

3. Purposeful reliance on doctrine mandates an imperfect but earnest commitment to make the system's ecology support the church's believing life.

4. Step Four systems encourage the parties' return to the earlier personal solution steps of Matthew 18 even while continuing to work with these members on creation of the dispute's solution. A system could also draw in whatever components from earlier steps which might enhance the parties' sense of responsibility for the eventual Step Four solution.

5. Preclude system inertia so that once a case moves to Step Four, it does not have to get stuck there. What principles and criteria switch off Step Four in the face of your denominational version of an "out of court" settlement, for instance?

6. Train your "reconciliators" (individuals, boards or whatever name you select) who are elected to implement your Step Four system. Not only does training lower your risk of the process falling back into the old Adjudication quagmires, but it is an important form of satisfaction support you provide these folks.

7. Harmonize your efforts to construct an evangelically-spirited Step Four system with the earlier Steps' personal solution and/or audication process. For example, preserve Audicators' integrity as you find it necessary for "reconciliators" to verify or retrace good faith exhaustion of the first three steps.

8. Clearly limit appeal of a Step Four system's decision. It should not be subject to review or reversal, for example, and you need to specify who can order a re-hearing (and on what grounds).

Afterword

More from uninformed good intentions than bad faith, most conflictors' attempts to "settle the matter" in one-on-one meetings end up as dialogues of the deaf. What next, then? "I am not going to meet with him (or her) again without a witness, because that is the biblical rule." Unfortunately, that is not the biblical mandate, at least when both of you are proceeding in good faith. This misunderstanding of what each next step is may be the most frequent reason why recourse to Matthew 18 so often ends in failure.

Redundancy and reinforcements for each "back-up" step are built into these six verses. When is more help from the church helpful for conflictors' efforts at personal solution, and what form can it take? When is it okay to have somebody else create the solution? When and how *must* personal attacks at church meetings be overruled? Although mandates for "excommunication" are not present in this text, how can we honor these verses in how we deal with our "back-door losses"? These are some of the issues I had to face in putting together this chapter.

5

Step Five: Reconciliation Ministries

A major emphasis to Matthew 18 is that no solution is valid if it does not point toward reconciliation within one or more of our One New Person relationships. Even when one "US" has died, others remain to be nurtured and cared for in our corporate and personal ministries.

For example, though a marriage may die through a Step Four divorce solution, intentional ministries are all the more necessary for the parties' life in their surviving Family, Parenting, Vocation, Neighbor, Friendship and Body of Christ One New Persons. Step Five calls our attention to what has to happen for peace-builders' *relationships*.

Textual Observations

Throughout our discussion of Matthew 18:15-20, we have been emphasizing its *redemptive* application. Sanctions [disciplinary] aspects of the passage are deliber-

ately being kept secondary in this book, as they are in
Matthew's eighteenth chapter. Below are some textual
observations about verses 18 through 20 of Matthew 18.

FORGIVE...AND REMEMBER NOT: VERSE 18

Throughout Scripture, this same action by God has
numerous expressions. "I will separate you from the sin
which I have forgiven, as far as East is from the West."
Or "I have cast them (away from you) into the depths of
the sea." God will bind up our wounds (Jeremiah 6:14).
And, "I will remember their sin no more." The key
doctrinal foundation for this action is "remember"
(*zakhor*) and "remember not" (*forget:* we contrasted its
modern counterfeits with the biblical view in Chapter
2).

Loosing—There is much less disagreement on the
meaning of *loosing,* whether in disciplinary or redemptive contexts. Quite simply, it is "forgiveness." We are
released from any obligation we owe, as from a contrac-
tual obligation or "debt" (*niddui,* as in the Lord's Prayer).
We should notice that the usages underlying this imagery emphasize that we ourselves incur these obligations and are responsible for them. We do not owe them
to Satan. Rather, we are so hopelessly obligated in and
of ourselves and we are so enslaved to these burdens,
that only God in Christ can relieve us of them.

The texts are not all that consistent on how this
aspect of *loose* may relate to the dynamics of verse 18, but
we would not be out in left field when keeping it in mind
or relating it to the *presence* of Christ (verse 20) as the
foundation for true Forgiveness in the parable which
follows.

Construction—In the original text's grammar, what looks like a mere technicality underscores *who* does the forgetting-and-forgiving. Literally, the text uses the future perfect periphrastic after an aorist: "Whose sins you bind *will have already been bound.*" So that when we forgive each other's sins, and when we *forget* them in God's name, God will have already forgotten-and-forgiven them!

Another scholarly point noted earlier underscores the primarily *redemptive* meaning of this verse: The "ban" (*menuddeh,* verse 17b) immediately preceding it *must* be immediately followed by a specified blessing. Otherwise, that ban is invalid. Everyone who heard Christ speak these words knew that, although it may come as news to us.

One final technicality: If the primary meaning of this verse were exclusively disciplinary, the grammatical construction would have to stipulate that the sin or obligation was being bound onto that *person.* In both John 20:23 and Matthew 18:18 the verbs used (*krateite* and *deomai*) imply neuter objects, "binding" onto something else—as onto the Levitical "scapegoat." However, because of verse 17b, neither can we swing to the opposite extreme of seeing only Gospel in all this. No, instead what we receive throughout this six-verse passage is both: Law *and* Gospel.

MAKE SYMPHONY: VERSE 19

"Again, I tell you that if two of you build symphonic relationships (*symphoneisosin*) concerning any and every practical issue (*pragmatos*) they may be pursuing, it shall be blessed (be ratified, succeed) on the part of my heavenly Father." That is a literal translation we have been noting.

Some attention was devoted to this verse earlier (in the Doctrine chapter). We keep referring to it since Scripture keeps pointing us to the importance of harmony, of making symphony in *how* we deal with our differences and disputes. Yes, how we cope with conflicts has eternal consequences for you and me. When we consider this aspect of verse 19 in the light of the parable which follows (the Unmerciful Servant), we must realize that, according to Christ, our personal salvation actually goes "on the line" in how we cope with our everyday conflicts!

Some of us suffer from a kind of Spiritual Schizophrenia. "I have my spiritual life consisting of my private relationship between Jesus and Me. Then, there is my practical life. Do not confuse them for me!" But it is encouraging to see verse 19 and learn that we become the heirs to an eternal promise when we stop separating our life that way.

It is a relief to know that we can claim and enjoy a Christian relationship with each other which is based on symphony rather than unison. We do not have to agree on everything to be *right* with each other. We can have many differences and still be bonded to the special One New Person which God created for us. We can experience this blessing with each other because that is the same way it is between God and us—rightly related, while still sinners. We can still live with our unresolved differences!

Making symphony is at once the objective and the starting point for how we deal redemptively with conflicts. God has already established us in symphonic relationship with each other. On that basis, let us go to work on our troubles with confidence which is founded upon what God has already accomplished between us!

THE GREAT PROMISE
FOR CONFLICT REDEMPTION: VERSE 20

"Wherever two or three have been bound together in my name, I am present among them." This is the *Great Promise* text in the gospels.

Let us see why that is so. First, we note several preliminary features. "Have been bound together," instead of "gather together": the word used in this text is a passive participle *(sunegnemoi)*. That means we do not achieve or do the gathering/binding/assembling ourselves. Rather, it is done for, to or *upon* us—we are "acted upon" by God's action. For example, the Bond of Peace (Ephesians 4:3) is not something *we* create but is created by *God*. This is a relationship to which we have already been bonded, and which we are required to express.

"In my name" focuses our motivation for Conflict Redemption at the highest level of aspiration. That is, we do not use Conflict Redemption chiefly for personal benefit, or to calm things down in the congregation's organizational life, or even because it is the Christian thing to do. Rather, it is done unto Christ! For Christ, in Christ!

The *"Gotcha!"* in this verse: all of Jesus's hearers knew a catechetical formula which Christ radically changes here. The old version went this way: "Whenever two or three have been bound together in *ha-Shem* (the "Name," which could not be spoken: JHWH, God's holiest name) to build Peace (or one of three other occasions which are not involved with this text [study of Scripture, to honor parents, to do deeds of charity]), the *Shekhinah* (divine Presence) dwells among them."

All the manuscripts agree on two crucial changes Jesus makes in this older formula. First, it is in *"my*

Name." Second, "I am present among them." We can almost see his listeners do a double take before their jaws dropped. It dawned on them: Jesus is declaring to them that "The Lord God of Israel and I am one in the same."

It is the most radical Christological claim ever announced by Jesus: He is God! That He does this in a passage about coping with conflict may not be that shocking when we recall that "ordination" for the new church included the authority to bind-and-loose (John 20:20-23).

No less important for us is that this declaration establishes the eternal foundation which verifies the *Great Promise* for Conflict Redemption: Christ is present when we do it in His name. Where Christ is present, true forgiveness is made certain.

Be not dismayed that this verse does not refer to sparsely attended meetings. There are other assurances of blessing for these. If we want to be clear in interpretation, however, know that this verse refers primarily to Conflict Redemption.

How high a priority does Conflict Redemption have for us in light of this verse? Notice that Christ promised his Presence in relation to three major functions:

1. the Great Commission and Baptism,
2. the Lords Supper, and
3. Conflict Redemption.

We do not know His reasons for this. We do know it is consonant with other statements He made. For example, in the "high Priestly Prayer" (John 17) and the John 20:20-23 passage, as well as Paul's listing the first "mark" of the true church as "being in the Bond of Peace."

Agendas: Reconciliation Ministries

At whatever Step solution is accomplished, intentional reconciliation ministries from the church are an urgent priority. Too rarely done anymore, they can be as productive and meaningful for your members as they are essential for the church's commitment to Conflict Redemption. (In most churches, that commitment is already stated in your constitution.) I would suggest that these ministries are of three types:

- **Affirmation of Reconciliation**
- **Christ-Care Ministries**
- **Expert Assistance**

Affirmation of Reconciliation

Affirmation of reconciliation is especially appropriate and desirable when solution has been achieved at one of the first *three* Steps of Matthew 18. The conflictors have created their own solution. That is something to be celebrated and encouraged by them, by others it affects, and by their church, especially when their preceding difficulties were well known by other members, neighbors and acquaintances.

Affirmation and celebration of reconciliation ministries should focus upon—

1. **Encouragement** of others to use redemptive strategies in their own conflicts.

2. **Regard** for these persons' renewed relationship. How do we now approach and relate to them since we no

longer need to walk on eggshells about their "thing," for example.

3. **Support** for their continuing efforts to sustain and strengthen their agreement in the Bond of Peace.

Modes for carrying out of reconciliation ministry include:

Symbolic practices—such as the banner mentioned earlier may be desirable. In conferring with the reconciled about what form or specificity any related announcement might take, do not be afraid to remind them: "Parishioners did know of the difficulty you were having. It is important that they know you were able to deal with it yourselves."

Ritual reinforcement—especially through use of a Bond of Peace Service. While the newly-reconciled are principal participants, you may consider inviting others who are specifically affected by the situation and/or a Peace-Agreement to witness this service.

Pastoral assistance—on any aspect of their Peace-Agreement which specifies brief or continuing support from the pastoral office. If the pastor is a party to the previous conflict, if there is a pastoral vacancy, or one or more of the reconciled is still alienated from the pastor, it may be best to obtain such assistance from another pastor with the specific approval of your Board (Elders, Deacons, Lay Ministers) and ordinarily in consultation with your Called pastor.

Never celebrate a tragic outcome, such as divorce or the death of another of God's One New Person relationships! If your eyebrows raise a bit at this, we mention it because several denominational groups actually encourage this biblically illiterate "fad."

Christ-Care Ministries

Christ-care ministries from members who know what it is like are vital for durable reconciliation within a troubled US, or for remaining relationships. This is particularly important when one or more newly-reconciled people may feel they are going it alone, are under some strain from their part in an Agreement, are growing weary, or even might be tempted to back out of the process.

Christ-Caregivers are not there as experts, certainly not as partisans. As personal Christ-Care is given, concentrate on the conflictors' role in Conflict Redemption and the process' blessing for them. Do not be surprised if a peace-builder initially holds to the Agreement out of spiritual fear.

After Intensive Audication, one couple told me that they had not dared back out the first day after the session because they were afraid "we would be sent to Hell if we did." The husband still retained an inflated sense of entitlement concerning his brother, which tempted him to renege on the Agreement. This became an agenda item for follow-up Christ-Care. It takes not only time but ongoing encouragement for a sense of blessing to override their initial fear.

Human nature being what it is, do not too hastily kick away even such an inappropriate prop lest they cancel their Agreement before it has a chance to take firm root and mature.

Christ-Care *must* not be confined to just one One New Person while neglecting the others. For example, if conflict has concluded with legal divorce, Christ-Care has to attend the parenting and family "US," which is now as confused as it is vulnerable to deflected stresses from the divorce. The divorced persons' Body of Christ and other One New Persons need intensive care lest they, too, become mortally wounded by this death of their marriage "US."

Expert Assistance

Expert assistance for implementing a Peace Agreement should be specified, if it is needed. For example, where finance and tax factors are involved, the newly reconciled should agree on whose assistance they will seek and when. Call in "experts" only when you have already created the basic solution. Called in sooner, the usual role of experts is to screw things up!

Any experts must pledge to *serve* the Agreement already reached, with no changes permitted! The only permissible exception to this basic principle concerns points which are illegal or in violation of a government regulation. If improvements and revisions in the initial Agreement become possible, the reconciled themselves must create them. This often happens, as their restored relationship strengthens.

When counseling or rehabilitative expertise may be another component for a maturing reconciliation, please underscore and reinforce participants' need to regard it as primarily done for the vitality of their One New Person *relationship* rather than merely for any individual's benefit.

Single Participant Reconciliation

What if one party to a conflict is dead, is long gone or refuses to take part in your congregation's reconciliation ministries?

> "My brother cheated me out of my inheritance and then died two years ago. How can I be reconciled to him, experience this forgiveness and forgetting you speak of, Jim?"

This man was especially distressed by comments on Christ's command to make our doctrines work between us (Matthew 18:35). Single-participant reconciliation is not only possible, but can be a rich blessing. That man's predicament was the occasion for developing the Individual Bond of Peace Service (see Chapter 15).

If efforts to include others are half-hearted or contaminated with avoidance, I urge prior private conversation with fellow saints to affirm your appropriate use of that Service so that efforts to include others are not counterfeit. The Individual Service is helpful for entering into a posture of forgiveness with that person whose absence has been a barrier to your desire to live in forgiveness with others. Do not go along with that "I have-made-my-peace-with-God-on-this" funny business to excuse neglect of good faith reconciliation initiatives.

There but for the Grace of God Go I!

A major obstacle to a congregation's commitment to put legs on Step Five is that our initial and superficial natural reaction to others' trouble can be: "Oh my, there but for the grace of God go I. It could happen to me (or to us)." Yes, of course, it could.

There is something terrifying for members of the
Body when a church member divorces, goes to jail, or
loses a job at age 59. It is devastating when two brothers
and their wives buy handguns to protect each one's
rights against the other over the family farm. Shall our
policy be to limit our ministry, support, encouragement
and Christ-Care only to the "innocent" party?

Rather than targeting their problems, we emphasize
how reconciliation ministries nourish One New Person
relationships and those bonded to them. The technicali-
ties of their problem are for them to solve. *Our* business
is to support and encourage them in their own efforts.

"Tripping over the Steps" of Matthew 18 need not
intensify conflict instances in *your* church, as it happens
in far too many others! As you live with this blessed
text, I urge that you remind each other to experience its
continued benefits by:

1. Being deliberate about the redemptive purpose of
   each occasion for its application;

2. Discerning how Law and Gospel dimensions of
   the text lead all of you in its proper use; and

3. Claiming its Conflict Redemption process in personal life and for your congregation.

Afterword

"Finally, that is over, settled. We shook hands on it."
But, is it over for your church's opportunity for ministry
to conflictors? For example, when divorce is the tragic
outcome of good faith efforts at Conflict Redemption,

other One New Person relationships are in dire need of our intentional ministry after that marriage died. Others, facing severe but still-private conflicts, need encouragement from their church if they are to venture into the realm of Conflict Redemption.

When a congregation takes seriously its opportunities for reconciliation ministry with conflictors, rather basic theological dimensions of this passage's latter verses open new meaning and resources for your church.

Two examples:

(1) Direct and purposeful use should be made of that usually misunderstood phrase, Bind-and-Loose.

(2) What is at stake when we try to deal with "back-door losses," especially when textual mandates for excommunication are *not* present in Matthew 18:15-20? Most important of all is the long overlooked "Great Promise" verse (20) where Christ not only clearly announces that He is Almighty God but establishes the sure foundation for living with each other in true forgiveness.

Review of the Five Steps
of Matthew 18:15-20

STEP 1: One-on-one, face-to-face meeting between you and the other conflictor, alone.

STEP 2: Use of Audicators

STEP 3: More help from the church

STEP 4: Third Party Creates Solution

STEP 5: Reconciliation Ministries

6

Obstacles to Church Vitality

$\blacksquare$

W hen I tell pastors that I work with conflicted churches, the most frequent unsolicited response is: "Well, *we* have no conflict at *my* church." My reply is "That's nice." You would think I had just implied that their faces were full of warts! Talking with lay people from various denominations, I find they respond differently. "We certainly could use some help at *our* church." The tendency of some pastors to be ego-defensive about the subject says as much about our churches as about such clergy. We will see why this is so.

Common sense tells us that every church has its warts and disagreements. If conflict has not yet erupted into open warfare on boards or in small groups, some members and pastors walk on eggshells wondering if and when it will. But they consider church conflict a dirty word; they are embarrassed about its presence, avoid discussing it, and would rather not deal with it. After all, many members come to church to "get away from it all."

One goal for *Peace in the Parish* is to enlighten Christians' attitudes toward church conflict. Conflicts are not occasions for judging who is right or wrong in some matter. That is not how your conflict with God works. Life in Christ is a daily Conflict Redemption experience. Right with God while still a sinner: *that* is conflict, with enormous stakes. But we place it all on this expectation: from that conflict will come eternal redemption! For Christians, *there* is the "model" and basis for Conflict Redemption in our lives together.

In the midst of conflict between God and me, in Christ I am redeemed.

Scripture teaches that the essence of everyday Christian living is keyed around redemptive conflict between God and us. Faith meanies nag me to lower my spiritual cholesterol levels rather than begin each day with amazement that I am the apple of God's eye, despite all that remains unsettled between us. In Christ, each of us is history's all-time biggest sweepstakes winner with an everlasting wealth we never earned or deserved. A pauper given a prince's birthright!

For a congregation, Conflict Redemption works like a theater screen on which is projected the epic story of living by grace in Christ—a story experienced by many Christians personally, but rarely corporately. But when we move from our individual seats to that screen and enter into that much larger picture together, we begin to know how the story should go for our church. When you know the story between God and you, you already know how Conflict Redemption works for your congregation. Simple principle, complex execution: the same *way* Christian life is for any of us.

After theater performers have learned their lines, one of the director's next steps is "blocking" each scene.

Performers walk through the mechanics of placements and movements. Although blocking is an important step for a worthwhile performance, it is *not* the performance.

So it is for us with procedures we see in Matthew 18 and suggestions given in *Peace in the Parish*. They are the mechanics, the "blocking" components. But the main occasion is opening night: working together on stage before a live audience, trying to draw them into the story. A story we know and are telling and doing. You are "in rehearsal" with *Peace in the Parish,* but keep looking beyond it to opening night!

Cut off from redemptive expectations, conflict becomes destructive, infectious, even lethal.

Remember the apostolic church! There were horrendous conflicts, power plays and jockeying for position. But the apostles got the job done! Their purposes were clear. They moved beyond their differences because of their mission. Others could tell what these Christians believed by how they treated each other, even treated their enemies, doing unto others as Christ does unto you and me. They could do the mission because they embodied its message toward those they knew!

Whatever its origins and contours, conflict's immediate impacts move along a range from discouragement and demoralization to dysfunction. Disputes smolder for years, until a short-circuit ignites a three-alarm inferno. Such destructive conflict roots in our self-centered and evil nature. It becomes the Deceiver's playground *and* his killing field, strewn with deadly booby traps and buried bombs. As with evil, suffering, and sin, Satan is the author of destructive conflict. But we do not have to let him be its publisher, nor do we need to continue following his script.

Ingredients in Your Conflict Recipe

Church conflict is always a unique recipe of *many* ingredients, most of which are present in virtually every congregation. There is no checklist of ingredients signaling that yours is a conflicted church. However, there *are* some predictable patterns blocking the road to church vitality.

Many conflict ingredients that may be disruptive in one congregation are no big deal in a healthier one. An analogy might be: for a robust man of 40, catching a cold is an inconvenience and irritation, but for his colleague who has had repeated bouts of pneumonia, the cold could prove fatal. So it is with church conflict.

These ingredients can be in the same pot for some time, even becoming smelly and rancid, without building up explosive pressure until: (a) something puts the lid on, and (b) something turns on the burners under what has now become a pressure cooker.

During the *Peace in the Parish* project, we put together a 50-minute videotape to introduce congregations to on-site consultations. The first few times it was used, members met me at the airport demanding to know who had informed on them because "that tape described what has been happening at our church." I had to include a disclaimer informing viewers that tapes were produced *prior* to my knowledge of their congregation. In other words, since the main ingredients of troubled churches are so common, be assured your church is not some side-show freak.

These conflict ingredients amount to obstacles to church vitality. They occur in otherwise diverse congregations. Several obstacles are chronic, while others are seen only occasionally. Only a few obstacles relate to immoral or deviant behavior, despite what the media reports. The most common obstacles involve:

- **Corrupt attitudes toward conflict**
- **Collapsed Purpose Systems** (Chapter 1)
- **Past is running amok** (Chapter 2)
- **Deflected distress**
- **Shoot-out meetings**
- **Bombsight Biblicism**
- **Theological Thugs**
- **Family Systems churches**
- **False doctrine in practice**
- **Hyper-dependency**
- **Codependency cliques**
- **Clergy immorality**

In explaining these obstacles, two caveats should be given:

1. Beware of the paralysis of analysis, of getting so engrossed with analyzing a situation that members are unable to begin moving on their journey toward vitality.

2. By all means, never use explanations of these obstacles to write off, demean or intimidate people.

ALL WE WANT IS SOME PEACE AND QUIET

"We do not handle conflict well at all! Conflict is an intrusion, an interruption and irritant in any setting, but it is particularly disturbing and unwelcome in our church! We just want peace and quiet at Bethany!"

Around its denomination and community, Bethany had earned the reputation of a trouble-making congregation. Even the parishioners began to believe it. It is as if some indelible graffiti had been spray-painted around the church walls: "Keep Out! Trouble-making Congregation Within."

What was the *problem* at Bethany? *Who* was causing all the trouble? Bethany's more active members were at a loss to figure it out. But it was as if Bethany's ship was dead in the water and the seas were getting rougher. They did not know what to do.

It is always a temptation to hear only noisy battles, while turning a deaf ear to the quiet sounds made by seeds of faith growing. Nonetheless, as problems emerged over the years, Bethany's members had traveled an easy detour: they blamed difficulties on an issue, a person or a faction.

Some members were content to merely hope things would calm down or to let bygones be bygones. But others wanted Bethany to do better than that. A few members sensed that the troubles were God's way of getting their church's attention. They knew that *if* they had higher expectations, God would turn their situation into a doorway to church vitality. Those expectations led them across that threshold, pointing their conflict toward the green pastures of its redemption.

OBSTACLES TO VITALITY

Corrupt Attitudes Toward Conflict

Virtually every instance of God's redemptive action and revelation happen in conflict contexts. That is the Good News!

The bad news is that our culture has conditioned us to have a corrupt attitude toward conflict. This attitude is a major reason for the litigation deluge which threatens to swamp everyday America. "Avoid it." "Get a smart lawyer to handle it." "Sue the bum" (rather than work it out face to face). "I will see you in court."

Centuries of civilization believed truth would emerge from *facing* our conflicts. But when the Me-Now generation in America erased *truth* and scratched in *winning,* most Americans learned a terrible excuse for what psychiatrists call avoidance. Got a disagreement? Get somebody else to handle it for you. As your first move, get a lawyer and file a lawsuit. However, in a healthy society, such a move can only be your *last* resort.

An historical principle stipulates that a healthy society regards personal or direct solution of conflicts as an essential foundation for national integrity. Trends that seduce citizens into abdicating that right and expectation are subversive, undermining our public contract. Too many of us scramble to give up this basic right and embrace such corrupt attitudes toward conflict.

"We will call in the District President (Bishop, Superintendent) to tell us which of us is right." "If Pastor Nauw stays, I am out of here." "How do we go about getting George excommunicated?"

With the possible exception of "E.T.," the last classic fairy tale was the "Wizard of Oz," which taught us that if you have a problem, you must deal with it yourself. But then came the "Marvel Comics" syndrome: Got a problem? Get yourself a Hero to cope with it for you. Get a:

Fixer—somebody else who will create a solution for this mess. It is human nature for conflictors to try to weasel out of the deal if a solution is created by somebody who does not have to live with it. *Fixed* solutions do not last. Those who have to live with the solution are much better off creating it for themselves.

Messiah—somebody who will save the relationship for you, your marriage, family, church. Pardon the pun but it is all too true: Messiahs have this track record of getting crucified. (This is a good warning to control our messianic-meddling temptations. "I was only trying to be *helpful*," you cry, as conflictors dump their cross on you.)

When you create the solution yourself, face to face, you are more likely to focus on your relationship than on the issues. Hence, Matthew 18:15 revealed this point: "...you have gained a brother," when you work through the issues face to face, "between him and you alone."

Judge—someone who will decide who is *right* and what is *fair* for each individual. Unfortunately, little regard is given to your *relationship*. Neither is a determination of what is *fair* based upon what each party actually can *live with*. Measured by just about any standard, bringing in some kind of Judge yells *"Failure!"*

SHORT CIRCUITS AT BETHANY

In Bethany's circuitry, I observed at least three forces at work in their attitudes toward conflict. These short-circuited any possible surge toward church vitality.

- **Avoidance**

- **Winning**

- **Issues Addiction**

Avoidance—Because of their unbiblical attitudes toward conflict, Bethany's members expected that nothing good could come of their strife. So they avoided dealing with it. Most members had been brought up with this outlook and never learned how to cope appropriately and effectively with their disputes.

Like many other conflicted churches, Bethany travels one or more of three avoidance tracks:

- *Fire the pastor* or blame the pastor for most difficulties. Pastor Nauw became the church's lightning rod, attracting high-voltage static generated from many other storms. "Our storms will go away as soon as we get rid of the lightning rod."

- *Tell it to the church* or, as the biblical ignoramus likes to say, "We need to get this thing out in the open. Put the issues on the table." If Bethany gives any authority to Scripture, 99 times out of 100 this notion must be ruled out of order. Only after the previous biblical steps of Matthew 18 have been exhausted *in good faith* (seventy times seven) are we permitted to go public with the complaint.

- *Maybe it will take care of itself, if we leave well enough alone.* This illusion was encouraged when several key dissenters left Bethany and things calmed down for a while. Know this: the weed seeds of one avoided conflict situation will be harvested a hundred-fold in later conflicts.

Winning—Winning is the measure of success in an argument, right? The opposite of winning is *losing*— something which appeals only to masochists. Today's chatter about "Be a Winner" and "Win-Win" solutions to problems deceives us about a basic fact of life: winners have a real knack for being the losers, in the long run. Paul tells us that "God chose the weak to shame (overcome) the strong." Paul reminds us of a fundamental historical reality. Those who think they are strong and successful resist necessary improvements, which might change conditions under which they became successful. Their creativity engines run out of fuel. By contrast, Paul's *weak* who live in godly discontent, sense how much better things could be. By-passing the winners slough with its quagmire of no-changes success, the weak take risks for better life which may not materialize or mature until the next generation.

Bethany had difficulty with wealthy families. Why? This trouble was rarely an issue with money, but rather was a product of their Winner's *attitude* which rigidly resists any change. This morning's wealthy Winners turn into this afternoon's Old Guard, you see. It can spill over into their church roles, especially when the members are *nouveau riche,* new money. Spiritual arteries harden when these folks succumb to power play stewardship: using or withholding their gifts to get their own way. To *win.*

Far too often, a winning outlook collapses a congregation's or household's Purpose System down to power plays and control games. Win-Win strategies for disagreements also rarely result in each party "winning" equally. If Jerry gains the same number of pennies as Mary does quarters, that is hardly a Win-Win outcome, is it?

Issues addiction—Related to the previous two forces, issues addition is the naive insistence that members stick to the *issues,* regardless of what it does to the living Body of relationships. Throughout Scripture we are told that how we deal with issues should be governed by our commitment to the health of our God-given relationships.

Christ promises in Matthew 18:19 "If two of you *make symphony* in how you cope with each and every issue (*pragmatos:* practical issue) your efforts will be blessed by my Father in heaven." It does not say you must play the same notes or instruments, nor does it imply that you must *agree* on the issues. But rather, make symphony in your One New Person relationships by bringing your differing notes, instruments and priorities into harmony. Symphony rather than unison: that is the biblical command we read over and over.

The prodigal son came home.

But his elder brother (the American issues-addict?) becomes terribly upset because he hears the sounds of *making symphony* coming from the house where his kid brother and his father have been reunited. You can almost hear him bellowing at them: "But you have not settled the *issues,* yet!"

So the father has to set the priorities straight: "My son...." That *relationship* is what has been restored here. Remember: the father ran down the road to claim the relationship and to reclaim "this son of mine," even before they dealt with the issues.

To speak the truth in love is a sublime thing.

The clear meaning of this statement is to get back on track our One New Person (Ephesians 2:14-16) relationships to which God has bonded us. But these relationships are threatened by what I see you doing. So I speak to you for the sake of our relationship's vitality, growth, integrity and nourishment. Speaking truth which kills is not of God. Truth which nourishes *is* of God! By the same token, we can be derelict in our Christian responsibility toward a brother or sister in Christ if we postpone speaking the truth to them for fear of giving offense.

The risk of giving offense multiplies if we approach the other party as an individual. Instead, we must focus our own mind and heart on one or more of those One New Person relationships. If we focus on what the relationship really needs, our strategy and message will rise above the level of each other's ego trigger-of-defense.

Take a hard look at what Bethany expects out of a conflict, beginning with who *wins*. Should your side be the winner or should the other side win? A better approach is to ask how your God-given relationships can win. How can each of you realistically claim the loser's posture so that your One New Person Relationships will be the winners?

HOW CAN WE HAVE PEACE AND QUIET
WHEN ALL WE HEAR IS LAW?

The interactive tension between Law and Gospel is as necessary as it has been difficult to sustain. As historians of institutions or movements have shown repeatedly, tension between Law and Gospel is not only a theological fact but is essential to the body's or system's integrity and vitality. Conflict easily disrupts that tension in ways which intensify our avoidance attitudes.

1. Conflict filters out the Gospel.

The more troubled a church becomes, the less Gospel is actually *heard*. The more personally distressed the preacher becomes, the more pulpit-thumping, fire-and-brimstone sermons will be heard. Pastors should not be praised for "telling it like it is" when those fiery winds blowing from the pulpit are stoked in the furnace of trouble at home, from the past, from frustration with church council, or from unseen addictions and worse.

Some parishioners in conflicted churches may say, "All we hear around here is the Law!" Often the problem is with the hearer. There is a rule of thumb: the more troubled Jack's relationship is with Pastor Nauw, the less Gospel Jack will hear when Pastor Nauw is in the pulpit. Jack will probably hear only Law, rules, attacks, snide cracks and negativism.

I have listened to taped sermons of pastors who were under attack. Usually what *I* heard were pretty good Law-Gospel sermons, especially under the circumstances. But the angry member tells me: "See? You heard for yourself. All Law!"

Contradiction between Proclamation and Practice

It is hard to get nourishment through a barricade. "We are just not being fed here," opponents may insist. This may be a power play, or it may be a legitimate complaint. Typically this statement arises from a personally experienced failure of the pastor's ministry and/ or of the congregational system's.

"How can I be fed by Pastor Nauw when all we got were platitudes and jargon the time we were having such awful heartache?" When Jack was going through difficult times, the *quantity* of time and effort of ministry was irrelevant because the *quality* came up short. Jack felt that what Pastor Nauw said in the pulpit was contradicted by the ministry that actually *happened*. (In the hospital, at a deathbed, during a middle-of-the-night trauma).

Barricades also went up for people who worked closely with Pastor Nauw when they saw an intolerable contradiction between Pastor's teaching or preaching and the way he treated church staff and fellow workers. *Practice cancels proclamation* for too many superb pulpiteers, including Pastor Nauw, who fantasized he was preaching the Gospel in all its truth and purity. He could kid himself on this, but he could not fool the saints around him.

2. Conflict generates a lot of Law.

A typical characteristic of disrupted congregations is a growing obsession with *Rules,* including patently legalistic job descriptions.

On the one hand: Historically and psychologically, an obsession with rules typifies a self-destructing system or person. Historians of ideological movements mark a movement's slide toward self-destruction from the point when the following two closely-related developments take hold: (a) rules for behavior or activism gain precedence over the movement's beliefs, and (b) an obsession with the language of oppression develops.

On the other hand: some rules are necessary in churches, but they should be *purposeful* rules. Rules are needed as a safeguard concerning such matters as non-member weddings, kitchen basics, communion practices and the like. But there must be a *purpose* and a shared sense of *why* for each rule in order to avoid invoking an offensive list of No-No's. The rules should be connected to *so thats* and flow directly from your shared sense of purpose. *Rules-driven* corporate behavior is radically inferior to *purpose*-led experience.

The Elders' Term

For more than a decade, Bethany talked about changing its constitutional provision which limited an Elder's term to one three-year stint, with re-election prohibited. Kurt, an old-timer, told me the provision was established 45 years ago to break up a gang of Elders who were on the Board "so long they thought they could run everything."

Last month, Kurt proposed changing that bylaw to: (a) two-year terms, (b) re-election could happen once with a full-term "sit-out" required before one could be re-elected again, and (c) staggered terms for better continuity. He was vehemently attacked.

Kurt was an evenhanded fellow. But his wife was an outspoken member of the anti-pastor group. So, members of the pro-pastor group labeled Kurt's proposal as a power play, insisting that his sole motive was to get rid of the pastor. Kurt shook his head in sadness.

Another version: Invent and ascribe great and griev-
ous sins behind the "other side's" actions. A crafty
strategy when done adroitly, but I have never seen it
done any way but clumsily in congregations. "Me-
thinks thou protesteth too much" is sure to dawn on
other members, who will be less convinced by the
validity of your indictments than by your dark-closet
motives in making them.

WHAT TO DO ABOUT CORRUPT ATTITUDES

First of all, Bethany's leadership needs to face their
own corrupt attitudes toward conflict. They can argue
over whose attitude is corrupt, or they can take turns
describing biblical episodes where out of a real mess
came new life, vitality, revival. From this perspective,
once you begin reminiscing about Scriptural episodes
you have heard since childhood, your own recalled
examples of this turn-about will far exceed any list I
could give here.

A word to pastors: when you try to "rightly divide"
Law and Gospel for sermons in a conflicted situation,
you must include the *situation* itself on the "Law" side of
the scale. The context is already generating so much
Law! Do not pile more on to it. Rather, err on the side
of Good News.

Since I am of Norwegian heritage, I tell a lot of
Norwegian jokes when working with a conflicted church.
The strategic uses of humor in church are considerable,
though often carelessly employed. I use humor to break
down Law obsession and to open members to God's
good news amidst their corporate migraine headache.

Corrupt attitudes toward conflict are never healed by trivial *positive* attitudes. Corrupt attitudes can only be transformed by redemptive substance.

Afterword

When I work with congregations, one of the things I do is to help them sort out what has happened. But, analysis becomes autopsy if there are no "so thats" permeating it. I used to tick off my list of chronic and occasional features of church conflict; others have their own lists. In my concluding site reports, "rank and file" members started taking careful notes when I began to make explicit what was always implicit--what needed to be done *so that* you can move toward church vitality. That is why this chapter and the next five have the overall heading: Obstacles to Church Vitality.

If reading these chapters makes you a bit uneasy because so many of the obstacles are already present in your congregation, there is no need to feel queasy. At least, not yet. Think of these obstacles as something like a wiring diagram. A church goes conflict-dysfunctional when several things happen to how it is wired: (a) a short-circuiting event [a Shoot-Out meeting, for example] overloads that wiring, (b) your family-system church bonding and leadership mechanisms cause a sort of congregational brown-out when faced with crucial energy demand, and (c) your collapsed Purpose System retards corporate discernment of least important from most important matters, intensifying confusion where your power sharks can go on a feeding frenzy. None of this has to happen! I hope the experienced suggestions included with these chapters will be useful whether your church is at or near the brink of conflict-dysfunction, or if there is still the chance to change direction.

7

Stray Bullets

A lso called the Kick-the-Dog syndrome, over-reactions usually transfer frustration or trouble from its originating battleground into an undeserving and unrelated context, such as Bethany.

Deflected Distress Reactions

Deflected distresses are the favorite fuel of over-reactions to a dispute or issue. We are all aware of household versions—break-up of marriage, parent-child alienations, money trouble, health problems and the like. But Bethany included an unusually widespread incidence of vocational distress. The matter is as often overlooked in churches as it is pervasive in American culture. Recent studies report that most—as many as 90 percent—of us do not like our work and find little satisfaction in our livelihoods. While vocational dissatisfaction dominates members' deflections onto Bethany, several corollaries of this distress clutter the congregation's pathways to church vitality.

Vocational Distress

Vocational distress can spill over onto a congregation with powerful impacts that are hard to overestimate. This form of deflected distress may originate from those whose retirement is resented, as well as from those still active in the work force. The loss of a job at any age is extremely stressful; loss of livelihood can match loss of life when it comes to household stress levels. Few congregations either recognize or minister to this need. Employees are devastated when they are terminated just prior to retirement and/or "cheated" out of retirement benefits. Perhaps an LBO ripped off the company pension fund, or a "bean-counter" mentality overruled fairness in management's higher echelons (the same folks who, in their next breath, whine about employees' lack of loyalty). In churches' profiles of "back-door losses" are many who found no purposeful support for their vocational distress.

For those who do not exit through its back doors, how do personal vocational troubles clog the Body's arteries at Bethany?

- **Compensatory Distress**
- **Trapped Distress**
- **Recognition Distress**

1. Compensatory Distress

Top Gun Tom

Tom gets dumped on all week long at his going-nowhere job and then by Lil, his overpowering wife, when he gets home. But once inside Bethany's big red front doors, he becomes Top Gun Tom. Oh boy, is he ever the take-charge guy over there! Take charge of the Pastor. Take charge of the Council. Take charge of the budget, the custodian. (The borders of his Kingdom were sealed off at the church kitchen, however, after he foolishly tried to reorganize the ladies' way of doing things in there. Of course, he does nothing with the Youth, except to crab that "we gotta do sumpin' about da yoot.") Each time Bethany's drive-train gets repaired, another of Tom's money-wrenches will strip the gears. Unless and until corporate priorities focus Christ-care on his vocational despair, Bethany will remain his private artillery range rather than his green pastures of satisfaction.

Then there is Janet, well-educated, talented and hard-working, from fair-skinned nordic background. She has already lost two deserved promotions to less qualified Minority people. Bethany's ministries ignore her vocational frustration and confusion. Should her vehement questioning of social concerns money and efforts that are focused on "oppressed" *minorities* really surprise anyone?

Some members at Bethany *do* understand that Tom and Janet are compensating through their obvious over-reactions to whatever is on the table. But most members are addicted to reaction reflexes rather than responding to needs. Tom and Janet are fellow Christians among you; they are not "issues" you react to.

2. Trapped Distress

Luther observed a distinction between *Vocation* and *Station* (or Job). On the one hand, I can have a sense that my line of work is gratifying and worthwhile, and that I am bonded to my calling in life in a way that is bigger than just me-plus-my-job. On the other hand, my current

Job gives me nothing but hassle and heartburn. Often, very real grief is generated when there are contradictions between my sense of Vocation and the actual Job I have. Work place dissatisfaction is multiplied when I feel *trapped* there, whether the trap roots from age, from dropping out of school to get that first set of wheels, or from no-way-out family obligations. No realistic alternatives are open to me. But if I also cover myself with Poor Me sackcloth, it feels like sandpaper when I rub people the wrong way, even at church.

3. Recognition Distress

People who feel trapped also tend to compensate with stewardship that mirrors a corrupt attitude toward their income. How can you get through to such people who regard their income as compensation for their level of job *dis*satisfaction. I remember an old UMW rule: the worse the job, the higher the pay. This job is the pits; that is why your pay exceeds the value of what you do.

"Whaddya mean, Pastor, you want a raise? Don't you like your work?" I hate mine, but you are supposed to *love* yours. That explains why I make so much more than you do, Pastor (teacher, etc.).

But, the more conflicted Bethany gets, the more strangled its "Satisfaction Wages" become. When you pay starvation wages on the Satisfaction side of things, there is no way your staff will feel they are receiving fair pay!

Our pastor is money-hungry! Very few are! Vital congregations do not make this complaint. You will hear this most often from those folks who are among the first to pull the chain flushing your church's Satisfaction payroll down the drain.

Relational Distress

Troubled marriages, parenting disappointments or "deflected aspirations" (i.e. living life through your children) can not only clutter the Body of Christ's circuitry at your church, but insert unsuspected short circuits. At least three impacts will become apparent:

- **Recognition drain**
- **Purpose System egotism**
- **Sexual distress**

1. Recognition drain

Recognition drain is especially likely from deflected aspiration parents. Their demands for recognition of their children siphon off the congregation's (Youth ministries, for example) available pool of satisfaction wages, leaving less for those who deserve more.

Marvin

The sanctuary was packed that Friday night for Public Catechization of this year's confirmands. I was making some last minute checks before going up front to put those kids through their paces. ("We are going to team up to *teach* them," I had said several weeks earlier. They liked that scenario.) Standing in a corner in the narthex were Marvin and his parents, non-members who attended every few years whether they needed to or not.

"Why isn't Marvin up there with the rest of his class?" his mother demanded of me. My jaw dropped. I had tried to get him into the class two years earlier but had flunked that attempt at route-of-entry evangelism. Each time I saw him in the neighborhood, I had tried another tack. No dice. *"Marvin?"* I found my voice. His father chimed in: "This is a big occasion for us. Even my boss is here." I beckoned to Marvin and drew him aside: "What is going *on*?"

Every Saturday morning for two years, Marvin left the house "for Confirmation class." But, every time he went bowling instead. We scrambled to finesse his parents' recognition dilemma; deals made (and kept, by the way). Next year, he was up there.

Did Marvin go on to seminary or to some such glorious outcome? No. He became a used car salesman, moonlighting as an Elvis impersonator.

Marvin's family was typical of several others in the congregation. These parents had fallen far short of their dreams in life, and they invested all those unfulfilled dreams in their children. Most of these youngsters could or would not make a profit from such bankrupt investments; they resented it all. But their parents' marketplace either included or centered on their congregation. Under the circumstances, it would have been easy enough to manufacture a kind of Funny Money to satisfy them. But it was more important to focus our attention on those failed dreams as an opportunity for ministry.

2. Purpose System egotism

Troubled relationships obviously shove self-confidence onto some rather shaky ground. Whatever the origins of distress, its deflection will weaken Bethany's Purpose System if an active member's motivation gets trapped in propping up his or her wobbly self-confidence. As soon as everything does not go just right in a claimed area of responsibility, this member will either make a frustration fuss or walk away from that project. Even leading a Bible study becomes an ego trip, instead of an opportunity to achieve higher So Thats.

Jerry

"I have to do this Bible study presentation at the convention," Jerry said. "It is my chance to regain my self-confidence."

The lowest purpose-level is driving him for now. What could or should it be? What is the range of So Thats for Jerry? Oh yes, here he is: talented, has a fine mind, a beautiful family, and a dead-end job. But there are some very old troubles with his late father and two brothers, presented by hard feelings over a modest inheritance. Jerry cannot let go of his growing-up menagerie of real and imagined traumas. In his fifties already, he has not achieved a tenth of his dishevelled potential. But now he can present his Bible study to all those people at the convention and feed his starving need for recognition.

Ego bankruptcy: but can Jerry do more than pay off those debts? He can, if he will connect this occasion to a specific system of So Thats! Fine: regain self-confidence. In terms of the Purpose System: *So that*...what? (So that it will help his home life go better, with Jerry being less crabby—*Level 3*) So that...what? (So that I can do this Bible study far less wrapped up in myself in order to help the audience gain useful insights into the theme's biblical content—*Level 2*) So that...what? (So that their closest relationships can grow in the healing power of God's Word—*Level 1*)

And then, it dawned on Jerry: "That highest purpose now puts my need for self-confidence in a different light, a much better perspective. In preparing for this, I seek that healing power in my own life, perhaps to speak to the group from this experience. Come to think of it, all this is changing how I will structure and format my presentation." And so the continuing interaction of So Thats with real needs and opportunities continues for Jerry.

Jerry's measures of success are no longer trapped in low-purpose self-confidence agendas. But, if roles of Bethany's members are pulled by nothing more important than "felt needs," motivation loses any real staying power until the temptation comes to change Bethany's name to "The Quitters Church" or "Wishful-Thinking Tabernacle." Members' roles need to be pulled into the electromagnetic tension between personal and corporate Purpose Systems.

3. Sexual distress

We are not referring to those who cannot keep their zippers under control, but to Christians whose relational distresses can spiral them down into acting out their sexual problems.

It is the height of folly to imagine everybody inhales a cloud of saltpeter droplets upon entering church, or that sexuality's allure while on church turf is limited to teenagers, non-members, or perverts. Most churches crave members' loyalty. That usually entails meaningful closeness and sporadically intense task-performance relationships. It may even call forth a singular harmony which may contrast with one's distressed relationships outside of church. Of course, much of it is not as deep or wondrous as we imagine.

Do not be surprised if these spiritually-veneered associations mire themselves in the genre of a psychological massage parlor if:

a) closeness at Bethany happens around *affinities* rather than *purpose,*

b) if response to "felt needs" is your easiest bonding mechanism,

c) and if there is no shared sense of *So That* pulling emotions to higher real purposes.

Drives prevail too readily in relationships which are not *pulled* by greater purposes!

OBSTACLES TO VITALITY

Over-reactions

1. Similarity reactions

"I do not like thee, Dr. Fell. Why this is so, I cannot tell. But this I know full well: I do not like thee, Dr. Fell."

"Joe, you really rub me the wrong way." Sparks fly between two Council members, regardless of what matter is on the table. There may be a more complex biography underlying these reactions, of course. But in this case, Joe realizes that his bristling posture toward Bob switches on because Bob's manner, phrases, attitudes and actions are so similar to those which irked Joe about his parents when he was a child.

2. Historical reactions

At Bethany and other congregations, Hatfield-McCoy types of tensions among extended families or kinship systems from way back spill over on the church. These tensions have never been dealt with, so other conflictors breathe the same atmosphere of perpetual recrimination. Bethany, the one potentially redemptive element with which all are affiliated, neglects its healing Conflict Redemption ministry with them.

Baggage on Mission-Start Takeoffs

Mission-start congregations have a special problem. Over-reactions can take the form of charter members' conflict history within their *previous* congregation. I have seen it too often: charter transfer members from other churches can include more thorns than roses.

Henry's Virus

Henry, more a fugitive than pioneer, brings a deathly virus into the new Body. Along with his transfer, Henry carries a bag full of horded hurts and resentments from his former congregation(s). The point is not whether Henry was at fault in his preceding church's troubles. His former pastor might be quite truthful in noting the transfer is a "peaceful release." The problem is that Henry's hurts were never dealt with or given up.

The pastor of this new mission congregation learned that Henry was not alone in hording hurts, so Charter Signing was preceded by a "Bond of Peace" service. (See Chapter 15.) The service followed the pastor's individual counsel and explanation of its significance to each new member. That occasion became a watershed—personally, as well as corporately—for all the new members. As they moved together into new mission and ministry, they were not stumbling over old and rancid garbage.

3. Transference reactions

Sylvia, a troubled member, is strongly attracted to the public role of Pastor Nauw, whom she perceives as having it all together. Her experience with this male figure at Bethany contrasts radically with her marriage and work-place relationships. Her sales executive husband is a bully; colleagues act like Gutter Groupies. No wonder she finds her pastor's public embodiment of right relationships so appealing.

As long as Sylvia also regards Pastor Nauw as a devoted husband and father, her relationship with him will likely continue to be a case of inspiration rather than seduction. Fortunately, Norma Nauw *never* calls her husband "The Pastor," and both of them visibly keep marriage and ministry in symphony.

Not so for the pastor at Nearby Church. While at seminary, an inexperienced professor had convinced the spouses of seminarians that the proper way to refer to their preacher spouse was "The Pastor." This professor imagined that doing do would support that pastor's authority. But, for the Sylvia's of this ecclesiastical world, doing so invited that pastor's seduction. Each time members at Nearby Church hear their pastor's wife refer to him as "The Pastor," amplified by the castrated cleric manner their public relationship affects, what gets *heard* is something closer to "Help yourself to my husband."

Historical and anthropological patterns can become too technical about "Ideological Hero" dynamics within a religious constituency. But something happens when a pastor shifts from everyday flesh-and-blood to Ritual Symbol. Whether your congregation is high church or has neither altar nor formal liturgy makes little difference. Or, if your pastor is the sort who has been known to conclude a Scripture lesson with (as I actually heard one do): "Here endeth the...*wrong* Epistle." Ritual is happening, symbolizing the way things *could* be for many of you—including a Sylvia or two.

Someday, harmony could happen; right relationships could materialize in Sylvia's life. She sees it happening up there at this service, symbolized visibly in flesh and blood. She wants to get closer to it and refresh her hope. If Sylvia experiences a healthy symbiosis between that Symbol and its visible marriage, parenting, family and friendships, then her agenda is nonthreatening.

If this sounds complicated, it is. But it does happen, more than we care to admit. Powerful relationship transference impulses go with the territory in church systems. Ignore that at great risk!

WHAT TO DO ABOUT IT:

First of all, recognize *why* personal distresses get deflected onto Bethany. I think the reason is fairly straightforward: distressed members perceive their congregation as an arena where they can somehow experience redemption from their tragedy. This should be a valid perception, to be sure. But if redemptive support or sensitivity are not forthcoming in times of trouble, members become angry and resentful. That resentment will be expressed in at least two common forms:

1. championing an issue with a passion which exceeds the issue's merits; and/or

2. over-reacting to any matter which directly connects to the role-person(s) who *could* have responded helpfully during this personal crisis. ("It is his [her] *job* to know why I am so upset.")

So long as Bethany's members *react* to an Issue rather than *respond* to the Person, the situation remains a dustdevil building into a tornado. I would urge Bethany to move into a concerted effort to teach their members how to become Christ-caregivers, so that people in need do not have to suffer their loneliness and tragedy alone. (Christ-Care is detailed in *Church Vitality* and our *Christ-Care* Bible Study.)

Pastor Nauw will begin to shine the spotlights on this urgent need for Bethany's members to become more caring in the same way Christ cares for them.

OBSTACLES TO VITALITY

Those Shoot-Out Meetings

Episode 1: There was a real shoot-out at the last congregational meeting. It started when Harold got up and said: "Mr. Chairman, I have several problems with this pastor." Among those members who left the meeting over the next hour were several who will never again enter Bethany's doors.

Episode 2: "Would you sign our petition to force the pastor's resignation? We plan to present it at the congregational meeting. Then we can call a pastor more to our liking."

Episode 3: "We would have less trouble around here if we would only follow the **rules** of Matthew 18!"

Each of these all-too-typical episodes violate the clear voice of Scripture, especially of Matthew 18:15-20. In example (1), if Harold was unable to verify that all previous steps of Matthew 18 had been exhausted in good faith, the Chair should have immediately ruled him out of order, before he even got into his complaint. Roberts Rules? The Chair *must* overrule them whenever their procedure violates either the spirit or letter of passages such as Matthew 18:15-20. *Must?* In this day and age, if the Chair and congregation ignore this counsel, the courts will not! Churches are losing multimillion dollar lawsuits over this kind of shoot-out your congregation *used* to get away with!

In example two, petitions have no permissible standing if:

- presenters cannot verify their good faith exhaustion of the prior steps;

- if equal accessibility to the petition was not openly offered to *every* member.

Example 3 demonstrates tragic lack of any understanding of Matthew 18.

Ninety percent of uproars at congregational, council and board meetings probably would not happen if congregations honored their constitutional commitment to handle such matters according to Matthew 18:15-20. So few of us have actually studied this passage enough to feel confident we can implement its spirit and letter. Shoot-outs are a chronic obstacle to vitality in churches where members or groups jump to the "tell it to the church" Step in place of repeated, informed, good faith recourse to the previous Steps commanded us in this passage. They neglect the text's objective of conflictors' *reconciliation* to their God-created relationship.

Your congregation's overloaded circuits have shorted out, and faulty wiring is overheated. An occasion like Harold's speech may seem insignificant in itself, but it flicks the switch: Shoot-Out! Sparks zap between certain members, and steam rises from those who are quiet. Whatever is pulling down your temple pillars, it is not Samson. What is going on here?

Look for some recent event or development that adds just enough to bring a festering situation to the point of critical mass. (As with atomic reactors: dozens of uranium pellet-filled rods are in place, but nothing happens until one more rod is added. The uranium reaches "critical mass" and chain reaction begins.)

During his interview, Harold revealed that early retirement had been forced upon him a couple months before the congregational meeting. But Pastor had been too busy to talk with Harold at the time he was notified of his "retirement." Harold had not reached the higher end of middle-management, so the high recognition and high achieving vocational success of his older sister and brother ate away at him. His angry statement at the congregational meeting made no mention of all this, of course.

Why were others' reactions typical of over-saturation at the meeting? About half the members there were anxious about family members who had just been "deployed" to Desert Shield, several of whom were in units trained to infiltrate deep behind enemy lines. To say the least, their emotional stress levels were on hair-triggers.

But these ingredients alone do not explain why the meeting's atmosphere was so volatile at the outset.

Look for underlying *systemic* susceptibility to shoot-out occasions. "Family-Systems" kinds of churches are especially vulnerable, given their basically emotional bonding-mechanisms and distorted leadership system. ("I have a problem with this pastor, Mr. Chairman" unwittingly places the congregation's house-of-cards system in jeopardy. It triggers reactions out of proportion to the merits of Harold's "case.") A purpose-bonded church will not be a stranger to occasional outbursts, but the Body will not be threatened by them. Your Purpose System provides a decisive frame of reference or perspective.

CARE FAILURE

More often than not, care failure will provoke outbursts which ride a different horse. How can you tell its breed? The attack's vehemence level exceeds the importance of the matter being expressed (whether or not you agree with its merits). The result is an overreaction. The visible vehemence will be closer to a level of intensity generated by care failure from church or pastor in times of personal crisis. Distress deflects onto the presenting issue or something on a meeting's agenda, a different issue from what is *really* wrong. Perhaps the church did some helping out, and that was appreciated. The problem originates from low-octane caregiving in times of high-octane crisis. Low-octane generic support group care is given without higher purpose qualities included.

When Harold's Identity purposes were assaulted by that forced retirement, the church needed to respond with more than fuzzies, welcome though a personal touch can be. Do not be surprised when Harold targets his church's Identity purposes level (which includes the Office of Ministry), even in wildly personal terms.

Neither should you be surprised when his Identity crisis pulls the rug out from under your corporate overriding purposes on this occasion, and everything collapses down to power plays and personal attacks. (This becomes the norm whenever a vacuum is created where your clear Identity/Message/Ministry purposes *ought* to be, and your Mission slides into such a mess.)

Coping with shoot-out situations:

I would suggest two strategic responses and a tactical one for these occasions:

1. **Strategic responses**

a) A priority is to *interpret* your church's Purpose System. "Let us keep this in perspective," at least. But remember: it is at such times that the congregation's *actual* Purpose System gets owned. Ownership broadens and deepens when members experience specific interpretation of their church's priorities in how people deal with Harold right then. Otherwise, it can turn into the old "fight fire with fire" fiasco, and parishioners depart the lifeless scorched earth that is left.

b) In supporting the Presider, leadership at the meeting has to *assert* the church's Purpose System. "We are having difficulty doing the right thing here. We also must do things right, according to our constitution's stipulation that such matters be dealt with according to Scripture. Harold, have you exhausted all the prior steps of Matthew 18:15-20, in good faith?" (Harold may insist he has.) "Who can verify to the Body that these members have, in fact, met together with fellow saints 70-times-7 on these matters?" *If* the chair can do so, refer the matter to a later point in the meeting (or declare a brief recess to gain the possibility for others to approach Harold on "what has really gone wrong.")

A helpful hint for when a presider's intervention is indicated: if television or the press handled the matter the way this is going, would they be vulnerable to prosecution for libel?

2. **Tactical response**

If Harold does not back off: "Harold, if it cannot be verified to this Body in its meeting that you have, in fact, exhausted all prior steps of Matthew 18:15-20 in good faith, I must rule your statement Out of Order." (Recall earlier suggestions at this point, Chapter 4.)

> **Caveat regarding Matthew 18 at Shoot-Outs: God forbid that these insights get corrupted into tyranny tools.**

While unity is a heavy objective laid upon the true church by Christ himself, goose-stepping conformity never is. Dissent, disagreement, vehement convictions, even anger, certainly are expected in the church of Christ. The key treasure to protect in volatile meetings, however, is the life and nourishment of our relationship in the One New Person which God created and to which He has bonded us in this time and place.

Afterword

Add it all up and it just does not add up: stated issues and the felt-heat level at church meetings are way out of balance. In church systems, this phenomenon of deflected distress usually exceeds by far what psychologists call "presenting issues" vs. the etiology of stress. (I have been a bit suspicious of faddish stress theory ever since the Toronto specialist who pioneered a prevailing theory died of stress.) Whether it is at a congregational meeting, council or one-on-one with him, why *is* Charlie so hot under the collar?

"What else was happening in your life when you left Bethany?" How often I have asked this question in interviews. You might be amazed by how many times I have heard responses which had nothing to do with reasons such folks gave you (or council members) for why they became another statistic on your "back-door losses" list.

Nine out of ten times I have gotten a "No!" to this question: "If you were going through tough times in your household, aside from some individual members, could you count on Bethany making it a top corporate priority to come through for you?" How would they answer at your congregation? So should you be so amazed that some members get so angry about their membership at your church?

8

Bombsight Biblicism

━━━━━━━━━━━━━━ ▭ ━━━━━━━━━━━━━━

What is Bombsight Biblicism? It is when—

- we drop Bible verses like cluster bombs on another person's actions or intentions. It is when
- we reduce Scripture to a deck of cards, as it were, playing with only half a deck, and too often dealing off the bottom. It is when
- we position ourselves as tyrants *over* God's Word instead of living *within* it. It is when
- we rip the living Word of God into little pieces, then mourn over why Scripture does not seem alive for us anymore. It is when
- we think the Bible is supposed to be brought *to* our situation, rather than the other way around.

If bombsight biblicism is tolerated or heeded in a congregation, it is a symptom of advancing biblical burn out. Alliances quibble over whether your set of verses is inferior to my side's collection of verses. Used in this manner, both sets belong in an ecclesiastical Side Show, a menagerie. "Come see the Bearded Bible Verse...the Stretched Text...the Hotheads' Hit Parade of Self-Load

Ammo Passages." If there is such a thing as heartburn in heaven, Paul must be guzzling Pearly Gates Maalox in frustration over how generations of pious conflictors beat each other over the head with misfit verses from his pastoral epistles.

"Is there a Benediction for this thing?"

Remember *Fiddler on the Roof?* One of Tevye's daughters marries a tailor. She gets a sewing machine, the first ever in that little village. Another new thing! There is that scene in her house when the machine has arrived and the townsfolk crowd in to see it. She asks the Rebbe: Is there a benediction for this thing?

Bombsight Biblicists would imagine she is asking him to bring the Tradition *to* this new thing, *to* the situation. Not at all! It is the other way around. The point of this delightful play: How can this new *thing* be brought into the...*Tra-dih-shunn*?

Bring the Cross to your burdens. Is that what we are told? Of course not. Bring your troubles *to* the Cross, *to* Christ, *to* His Word if you would experience its healing power.

Biblical scholar or new Christian alike: to live within the Word precludes imposing our private agendas *upon* the Word. Learn how to live *within* the Word, lest we rob ourselves and others of hearing its clear voice amidst our troubles.

Critical Methods of Biblical Scholarship

We do well to discipline our study of Scripture, using the best methods and research available. How do we know when that scholarship is beneficial? When it safeguards against our reading into the Bible what is not there, against super-imposing some scholar's agendas or our own upon the text.

Some of the most vehement attacks on various critical methods used in biblical scholarship have come from the worst Bombsight Biblicists. Their use of Scripture elevates their own authority *over* the Word no less than some "scholars" try to do. Disguised as interpretation, both extremes tend to be literalists, crippling the text in bondage to itself in order to increase their private authority *over* it.

Both extremes' methods do not stand up well under competent scrutiny from other disciplines. As a historian, I have to shake my head at what some still try to pass off as "historical" criticism. Why? Because their operative understanding of historiography was discarded by mainstream historians generations ago. For example, the question is posed by some: "Did the Resurrection actually happen?" Tested by modern historical standards for evidence, it does qualify as an "historical" event.

From historical critical methods, we applaud recent insights which have helped us cast aside the poisonous anti-Semitism that blinded Biblical studies too long. Thanks to continuing research, we are getting a better handle on what first century Jews *heard* when they were in Christ's presence, as well as what those people expected to hear, but did not. We can begin to appreciate the impact of so many stunning "Gotcha's" in Paul's epistles!

To hear and receive clearly the living voice of *God's* Word, we have to clear away the clutter and hidden agenas shutting us off from that voice. We shun both extremes of biblicism and criticism in disciplining our Bible study to this sole end.

Versions of Bombsight Biblicism

However it surfaces and works in other settings, Bombsight Biblicism appears at Bethany under several disguises:

"Published Proof" Biblicism

Published Proof Biblicism means trying to prove *we* are in the right on this issue. In my interview with a gentle old saint, Hans shared his concern about the associate pastor's disregard for any need to know the flock. Quite obviously, this pastor's Divine Call must have come from the Pharisees. To defend his barricaded little clergy universe, he had arrived with a shiny new seminary AK-47 fully loaded with Dum-Dum bullet Bible verses, with the safety Off.

They are doing it to us again!

Pastor Withit, Bethany's associate pastor, is livid. "They are doing it to us again, Marcie. The same as every place we have served." If anything, Marcie is even more upset than Withit. She had worked hard to help him through seminary, a real partner sharing their sense of Call into the ministry. As in the previous two Calls, Harry had come here with a comprehensive Program in hand. It was the latest and best stuff from seminary for turning a church around. (He had spent a lay-off [severance paid] quarter there before Bethany called.)

Soon after they arrived, both became frustrated by lay leadership's foot-dragging on Harry's ideas. Both of them jaw-boned members. Harry and Marcie used every forum and vehicle they could to communicate The Program's merits.

Then, came tonight's Council meeting. Even sainted old Hans, an Elder both of them loved, had not supported them in the vote: "Pastor, how can we get behind you on these things when you do not know us yet?" What now?

Marcie wrote two letters and sketched out a third. She worked for days on them; one was to the Board of Elders, another to Council. "These are not *attacks*, Harry. This is *teaching*, to open their eyes to how *right* you are." She has a good memory. She listed every comment reported by Harry about the Board's discussion or action bearing on Harry's program. Then, she bombarded each item with Bible verses.

As to Elder Hans' comment, she fumed: "Our Pastor's Call is not to be chummy, but to do Word and Sacrament ministry. Period!"

"Are you better than Jesus, Pastor?" Hans asked when he came alone to the office. "He went among the people, got to know them so well, healing and helping them where they lived and worked and wept. Surely, ministry in His name cannot forsake His way of doing ministry, Pastor."

Following Marcie's Bible dive-bombing assault, verse-citing newsletter articles and petitions of varied stripes circulated throughout Bethany. Whatever validity their case might have is not the point. Rather, it is their twisting of Scriptural authority to serve partisan agendas.

Confetti Biblicism

Confetti Biblicism means adding a pinch of biblical tidbits to season any situation. As inspiration and encouragement to Christians' daily life in Christ, favorite verses are a blessing. That is not what is going on with Confetti Biblicism. Rather, we are speaking of—

• Counseling which rattles off a batch of verses at troubled or distressed clients, without interpreting a text in ways which help them bring the situation to God's Word for insight, healing and direction.

• Teaching or preaching which fosters an illusion (from the pulpit or on your television screen) that the message is centered in a specified Bible text when, in fact, the text is only a pretext flag waved over whatever the teacher or preacher *feels* like saying.

• Variant of Confetti Biblicism: the Pot Shot version. Indiscriminate pot shots aimed at other conflictors' attempts to express sincerely-held opinions on matters which, on the face of it, have no biblical relevance. Relatively trivial matters such as landscaping the church grounds, deciding what color scheme belongs in the Fellowship Hall, and wrangling over the new sanctuary carpet can consume too much of Bethany's decision-making energy. I have *heard* Potshot Biblicism ventured to sway such decisions.

Holly and the Nerd

John not only had acne on top of acne but a personality to match. He was the sort of fellow who never got a nickname. He would go up to a cluster of new girls at a rally and begin: "John's the name. I'm saved, sanctified, single, and searching." Yuck! Undaunted, he was relentless in pursuing what he called his Divine Crush. Holly was her name, the premier yum-yum of our era in Luther League. Soon she had enough of his greenish-toothed pursuit and read him off with a specific catalog of Why-I-Won'ts.

John knew Holly cherished her Bible. He countered each of her reasons for turning him down with *two* Bible verses in writing. He would quote such passages as Isaiah's prophecy about "no form or comeliness in him." To which she added but one reply: "so he opened not his mouth. Verse 7: check it out, John."

Alternatives to Bombsight Biblicism

Alternatives to Bombsight Biblicism and Biblical Burn out at Bethany amount to a change of *posture* rather than a change in programs; a change of *intent* instead of a change of information; a change of *eyesight* rather than change of expertise.

Our Posture Within the Word

Pastor Nauw will be placing a new emphasis upon the Christian's biblical posture! We stand *within* the Word of God. Paul's key principle was: "*in* Christ." *Under the Word* language can convey a sense of detachment or of separation from the vitality and dynamism of God's Word. The more accustomed we become to being *within* the Word, the less tempted we will be to climb on top of it.

We need to stand *within* the whole life and voice of Scripture, not amidst the scattered debris of half-used fragments. The way some of us relate to Scripture reminds me of how some teenagers maintain their room: clothing strewn about, a potpourri of stuff taped to the walls.

Something of Nerd John lurks in all of us, especially when we are tempted to use Scripture's pages for building stone walls around ego. There are some who imagine they are at home in Scripture whereas, in fact, they are in prison. Or, is it a zoo: "Step right up, folks. In this cage we see the common self-righteous ego bird. Two things make this breed interesting. While in captivity, it feeds itself a strict diet of Bible verses, much like that Panda over there devours bamboo shoots. Second, it keeps wrapping itself in the skin of a Christian. They never last long because they turn into mummies under each layer of decaying skin."

Scripture certainly is neither prison nor zoo. It resembles a health care center whose healing forces draw our wounds and afflictions unto itself again and again. If we bring our burdens to God's Word and to the Cross, our eyes and lives will be opened to that Light which now can illuminate more of those dark tunnels.

Bridging Head and Heart

Bethany comes alive in God's Word as members experience His Word in traffic between Head and Heart. We grow into vital Bible study as we outgrow childish, information-addicted "what I get out of it" notions and instead focus upon *purposeful* Bible study!

Some of us have moldy habits of caging Scriptural information in our heads. Others are inclined to filter out those aspects of Scripture which seem too intellectual and cherish only those parts that speak to their own experience. How may Christians grow beyond either extreme?

- "How does this *work?*" the more conceptual/doctrinal person must keep asking. *That* is the recurring theme of the classic catechism to be learned. How does this text help me? How does it educate me in helping him or her in times of distress?

- "What does this *mean*?" those who are more experientially-centered must ask, to be free from their spiritual ego-centrism. *So that* I can do unto others as Christ has done to me. *So that* I can explain to that troubled dear one how the Gospel heals with precision and effective power. *Articulate* compassion surely has to be one urgent reason for Bible study!

- The extent to which *we live within God's Word for the sake of others* can change both types (Head Christians and Heart Christians) into Head-*and*-Heart Christians.

- If this is our intent, to live within God's Word for the sake of others, the seed of God's Word finds deep and fertile soil indeed.

WHAT DO YOU SEE IN A BIBLE TEXT?

1. Text as Kernel of Grain

Some Bible readers see texts as tidbits of grain whose husk has to be peeled off to get at the kernel, the meat, the inner meaning. At one extreme, this imagery was typified by notorious "demythologizing" among followers of Rudolf Bultmann, who lacked their master's evangelical center. More commonly, however, this view is encountered in what might be called the simplicizing school: reducing each text of Scripture to a single point.

For example, each parable is said to focus on a single teaching. (The less you know about ancient rabbinic *aggada*, the more likely you are to buy into this fallacy.) Or, somebody imposes on our understanding *the* interpretation of a certain passage, implying this is the only way to see it for all time. (For me, among the most offensive are those uncommonly strange *Book of Revelation* Bible teachers who know nothing about John's audience of distressed Jewish Mysticism. The "Heavenly City," Temple, Beasts and so on were all well-known themes which John redirected so they pointed to Christ.)

2. Text as Jewel

During the time of Christ and the Disciples, a preferred imagery regarded each text of Scripture as a *jewel;* specifically, as a sapphire. Its worth is seen in how many brilliant lights radiated from it. The more lights, the more valuable a text. No matter how few lights it seems to radiate *now*, every word, every text is a precious jewel. Furthermore, as one moves through life and around that jewel, new lights radiate from it, lights *you* never saw before. Interpretation can never be locked in; it must be kept alive.

Since, at any one time, the brilliant lights can be seen clearly only on one side of that jewel-text's triangular cut, *interpretation* can only be ventured in concert with at least two other masters of the tradition. Individual study was expected, but *not* teachable interpretation by any solo individual.

What was the light's source? The jewel-text was radiating lights refracting from the Presence (*shekhinah;* also "splendor") or Name of God. Only the fool would value the refractions (interpretations) over the jewel itself. Only the fool would value the jewel more than the Source and Giver of its refracted Light.

Quite a picture: Bible text as *Jewel.* It is at once humbling to scholars trapped in their conceits and to pompous babes of faith who glory in their fixed ignorance of other facets, other lights radiating from the jewel. What do *your* members see in your favorite Bible passages: kernel or jewel? As members move around their own less favorite passages, can they see new and brilliant lights they never saw before?

Theological Thugs

Most denominations have them: gangs of clergy and/or laity who prowl the larger church under diverse Flags of Convenience. While doctrinal concerns flags and advocacy flags come readily to mind, other causes can as easily serve such folks' need. While their campaign wires into concerns honored throughout the church's mainstream, these partisans' energies and satisfactions are heavily driven by autobiographical distortions.

We have considered how disruptive such matters can be for a congregation. But they leave as vivid a trail in larger denominational contexts, too. It is tragic to see how these militants gang up on their regional or national denomination to divert it from outsurging mission mandates given by Christ!

Many of these people are ACOA's. Since childhood, they have craved allies. They crave control and reinvent what actually happened in order to "make it all better." These are survival techniques carried into adulthood. They are easily flipped over to put the worst construction on other people's motives and actions. In church politics, they tend to treat elected leadership as they would their own dysfunctional family-of-origin leadership. "I was wronged by my parent(s), which entitles me to do *you* wrong, especially when it serves to bring church-wide matters under my control."

Defrocked Pastor Bert

Bert is an ACOA, a former church college teacher, as was his father. When he came to be pastor of this congregation, Bert reserved his primary ministerial energies for codependent sectors of the membership. Finally ousted, he fled to his third wife's home ground, into a different jurisdiction of his denomination.

· Without Call, Bert immediately began rounding up other codependents under his flag of doctrinal orthodoxy. His explicitly strategic focus was to get even with that jurisdiction's elected head, even though he had had nothing to do with Bert's life.

Betty: the Emblem

Betty is a lesbian and an adult survivor. An avid advocate of inclusivity and a talented organizer, she was nominated for an elected leadership post in her denomination. Most of the active supporters seemed motivated by heartfelt concern over the role of women in the church.

Betty played on that concern, maneuvered to become its Emblem in this election. But that alone does not win church office in a constituency which retains something of a yearning for larger mission and overriding purposes. Her core network, at least six of whom are ACOA's or adult survivors, launched a behind-the-scenes campaign of blunt intimidation. Thugs, no less than Bert's Boys are!

It is easy to find some Flag that many well-meaning folks in your denomination will salute. Bert might convince himself he is a genuine citizen of that Flag's domain, especially when his cause helps bring his chaotic autobiography into a semblance of order.

Betty's Flag may draw a loyal group. But what about unwitting prospective allies of her agenda? What should the rest of them look out for? Two clear principles should inform our discernment:

1. Is the cause this candidate or group espouses truly embodying the larger mission of our denomination? Why do they want control? To what Christ-centered, world-redeeming end? Is how they are going about this campaign embodying *in fact* what we believe? Is their procedure within the authority of God's Word in Matthew 18:15-20, for starters?
2. Is their cause the core business of Christ's Body? I have noticed several denominations that have turned into ecclesiastical schizophrenics. On the one hand, they have their uncommonly self-destructive Convention or political mind set. But that same church in Ministry is about the core business of God's People. Same folks. Personally they know better, but put them in a convention mind set, and they seem to take leave of their senses!

Ask yourself when your vote is solicited: Is this why Christ died and rose again? There are countless souls to be saved and hurts to be healed. Is this what these campaigners are furthering? If not, despite their crafty knee-jerking vocabulary and flag-waving, you probably are getting "hustled" by Theological Thugs.

Fortunately, their kind will not prevail in Christ's Body. Maybe for a time they will intimidate an ecclesiastical bureaucracy, but only for as long as the rest of us are not wise to their game plan, its shadowy origins, its corrupting purposes.

Doctrinal Storm Troopers

I worry that a spreading ooze of what George Gallup, Jr. calls "faith illiteracy" is suffocating the long-term integrity of America's churches. That ooze is encouraged by a breed of fellow travelers with Theological Thugs called Doctrinal Storm Troopers. What is the difference, and why does it matter?

Those thugs have credentials. Often good theologians, they have paid their dues, academically and professionally. When waving Scriptural and doctrinal flags, they know the substance behind the symbol. The Storm Troopers, on the other hand, lack credentials in the larger system they would tyrannize. In a word, they are misfits (not unlike their geopolitical-military predecessors of not so long ago).

Recognition Craving

Bill had never gone to church until his cataclysmic conversion five months before he entered seminary. The first of this extended family to finish high school, his college degree just was not producing enough recognition to satisfy the family's craving. So, not surprisingly, Grandma also paid his way through seminary where his classmates regarded him as quite moderate. Unfortunately for Bill, most of his denomination's clergy roster had deep-rooted relationships from way back, for generations.

What was an ambitious fellow to do? Bill had heard that returning missionaries were held in some awe. Off he went with his wife and children to the mission field. He served his term. He anticipated being one of those returning heroes. Instead, he was recognized by his denomination with a Call to serve a parish in one of Wyoming's least famous communities.

Bill developed a keen interest in several militant publications whose spiritually salacious audience is his denomination. He became angrier over where his career has dumped him. The last straw was when his uncle identified his location as Cattle Rustle, Nevada.

Bill wrote heated letters to the Editors. He was contacted by other low-recognition colleagues, one of whom finessed a bail-out Call for him. Later, the network maneuvered him into a fairly sizable parish on the Plains, where he lasted only a few months. His over-saturated anger, frustration and frantic lust for recognition simply took over Bill's career.

Bill's profile and vocational history parallel those of most denominations' Storm Troopers, doctrinally saluting or otherwise. Since vocational frustration among today's clergy is widespread, it is surprising such militant groups have not enlisted more recruits. Percentage-wise, back-door losses among clergy rosters already exceed those of some denominations' lay membership lists. Many other pastors are as modestly equipped as Bill, but they carry on such faithful and satisfying ministries. None of *them* are Storm Troopers. Why not? Key differences seem to be that they do not share Bill's suffocating anger or his malignant need for recognition.

What can be done? Andy Warhol's panacea for what ails the nation was to fix it so "Everybody gets *famous*— for 15 minutes." This might help a little. I suspect solution to such a widespread dilemma will have to rely on restoring collegiality to our clergy rosters. However, a recent trend in America's denominations is this: clergy have become *competitors* more and more, *colleagues* less and less.

The intense loneliness and isolation by clergy parsonages in conflicted parishes is devastating. "To whom can we go, talk to?" they plead. A few flee to CPE (Clinical Pastoral Education). Instead of using CPE training for skill building, it too often becomes a support group substitute for collegiality.

I am not sure how clergy colleagues can satisfy Bill's excessive hunger for recognition. But this hunger might diminish as colleagues help him deal with his accumulating anger, to let go of it, to rely personally on the same doctrine he would so staunchly defend.   Colleagues have to target Bill's areas of low self-confidence in ministry. (Usually we are most flexible in those areas in which we are most confident, while we tend to be most rigid and authoritarian in our weakest areas.)

Why colleagues? If some of them are among the more doctrinally and theologically competent, they can assist Bill in building his own bridges between Head and Heart, between doctrine known and doctrine done. Why? *So that* he could move on with satisfying ministry and resign his commission with those Storm Troopers.

Afterword

Christians who used to delight in the healing power of God's Word get caught up in a congregation's dissension and lose their biblical marbles. Pastors and spouses, members who ought to know better hurl proof-text letters at Council, Elders, every-member mailings and bulletin boards. They are trying to make the Bible jump through private agenda hoops until it is clearly your word against God's.

On the other hand, I usually find that the authors of such misuses of Scripture actually resort to these diatribes because of an underlying personal confidence in and commitment to its authority for their lives. But, what do those episodes do to the integrity of biblical authority in your congregation and to your need to be sustained within God's Word for the sake of others? This chapter leads toward an effective yearning for *purposeful* reliance on God's Word.

9

All in the Family

◻️

Most plateaued, declining or conflicted congregations place high importance on being like *family*.
So do cults! In fact, most cults are deliberately organized
as family systems.

What is so bad about that? After all, Scripture talks
about the family of God. We can leave it to scholars to
debate whether the phrase is *definitive* or only *descriptive*.
However, in Scripture the phrase is a small tail on a
much larger dog because so many more important
things overrode the apostles' family analogy for the
church. Problems come when the tail tries to wag the
dog—when a family model takes on inflated importance. That is what happened at Bethany.

"We have not done that here," is the usual response.
"We are about much more important stuff." In my
experience, the latter claim rings true for most churches,
but more like wind-chime tinkles than a pealing caril-
lon. A short Church-Family Checklist can help rank just
how problematic that family feeling may have become
for your congregation.

Family Faux-Pas Checklist

1. Do your lay and clergy leadership *bring* more energy to their roles than they get back?

2. Do you hear, "We have always done it that way" as a common rationale in decision making?

3. Beneath appearances, including race, are your most active members quite similar in the priorities they place on education, in how well they grasp concepts, in their style of religious experience and/or expression, in the value they place on home and family?

4. Does most of your active membership seem to prefer *strong leadership* from pastors and presidents?

5. Is there considerably more *talking* about evangelism than *doing* evangelism?

6. In determining whether you have the right pastor, are the qualities that members *like* about your pastors more decisive than how effective the congregation's ministry is?

7. Do the congregation's best attended and best supported non-worship events have a strong sociability component?

8. Has there been a long-standing tendency for members to blame the pastor when things are not going the way they should for the congregation?

9. Are most of your small groups comprised of like-minded or otherwise fairly similar members?

10. Does it seem that most of the congregation's attention, resources and energies focus on keeping the church going and growing?

While good things can be said for each of these checklist questions, together as pieces in a pattern they become markers along a road to decline and trouble. Red flags should start waving if your answer is *yes* to any five of the above. The closer you get to *yes* for all ten, the louder the alarms should sound. Why? Because there is a history and a reason behind each question.

Despite recent widespread fascination with family systems theories for the church, a family feeling can build four time bombs which blow up bridges leading to a vital church system. These time bombs are ready to explode at Bethany.

OBSTACLES TO VITALITY

TIME BOMBS
for Like-a-Family Churches

Time Bomb #1: "Ties that Bind"
Time Bomb #2: "Take Us to Your Leader"
Time Bomb #3: "More Drain than Gain"
Time Bomb#4: "We Have Always Done It That Way"

Time Bomb #1: Ties that Bind

Do the ties that bind produce a negative or positive effect? A major characteristic I track in working with congregations is this: What glues things together here— relationships, authorizations, groups, decisive priorities and the like? A trouble-prone church usually associates around a combination of gut level feelings and activities. Its bonding mechanism is *emotional*.

"We have the right pastor now because I like him, and I like how he does things." Pastor Nauw has a pleasant way with people, and that is a blessing. This asset becomes troublesome, however, when nothing more important overrides it in deciding when or if Pastor Nauw is doing a good job.

However, from Pastor Nauw's point of view, being *liked* became the locomotive rather than one of the cars on his Ministerial Train. Quite likely he will become emotionally and spiritually destitute before long. Why? Because the energy needed to pull the whole train is taken from *his* spiritual and emotional reserves, without being adequately replenished.

"We left Bethany and joined First because there is so much more going on over there. Bethany just cannot meet our needs the way it used to." Look at Bethany's Annual Reports for the past decade or so: lots of activity (we did this and that, raised x-number of dollars, elected so-and-so as our officers, and oh-my-are-we-short-of-money), but no *So Thats*. Bethany is running out of gas because it has been siphoning fuel to fill its own tank from members' personal reserves.

By contrast, Ties that Bind a vital church are *purposeful* ties. Purpose bonding is a key difference between congregations that are alive in the Body of Christ and churches that have deteriorated into the Busy-bodies of Christ. "Our hearts in Christian love" becomes a purpose bond when together we can help others come to know and grow in Christ.

Activities, personal nice feelings of family-like ties at church become durable blessings when we tie them to a verifiable system of specific *So Thats*.

Revisited: Four Purpose Levels of Motivation

We do pay attention to how members treat each other so that (Level #4) people will enjoy it here, and so that (#3) things will run smoothly at church, and so that (#2) we will express our growing maturity in doing unto each other as Christ does unto us. Our *most important* purpose for doing this is so that (#1) others will come to know Christ and follow Jesus throughout maturing expression of purposeful reliance on doctrine.

Time Bomb #2: Take Us to Your Leader

"What we need around here is strong leadership." Do we need a patriarch or matriarch cult leader perhaps? Are we to assume that to have a strong church, strong leadership must come from the top?

Usually it does come from the top in families: parent, grandparents, relative, eldest child. Churches got by with that sort of leadership years ago when clergy were much better educated than most lay members, but we have seen a massive increase in the competency levels of the laity in most churches. Notions of from-the-top leadership go tock-tick in today's real world.

To keep abreast of what is happening in church members' Monday's world, I do faithfully what I urged upon my seminary students: read business magazines. Pastors, if your congregation is in a rural area, keep current with the farm or ranch journals and trends in small business. It is dumbfounding to speak with so many vocationally ambitious Christians working in companies committed to "organic management" models who, in their church, remain stuck in leadership assumptions their own companies threw out. Career future depends upon their tuning in on new principles of management. Why do they take leave of these principles once they walk into church?

Trinity's Shepherd—Pastor Tim

Trinity's pastor was still several years from retirement when he became ill from a rapidly-deterio-
rating case of emphysema. For years, Pastor Tim had
done everything at church. His *over*-functioning
enabled the congregation's *under*-functioning. In
effect, Tim was the church's eldest brother. He had
accumulated most of its responsibility, and he had
authorized whatever tidbits were accepted by laity.
They meant well in calling him a real Shepherd.
What this also implied was that, as Sheep, members
were incapable of handling responsibility.

Those last few years of Pastor Tim's tenure saw
members taking on more and more responsibility.
Because of his illness, there were times when he could
barely make it through the service. Parishioners
discovered they could do the right things *and* do
things right. When Pastor Tim retired, this new-
found lay initiative and responsibility blossomed
during Trinity's vacancy period. In effect, Trinity
was outgrowing its old family-system model of leadership. Even long-dormant plans for a major building program came alive again during those vacancy
months.

Trinity then called a new minister who was not a
typical Herr Pastor. When he arrived, he was a
walking casualty case of hurts from previous congregations. Old wounds quickly turned him into a Saturday Night Special: shooting from the hip and
quickly overheating. He had virtually fled his previous church where things had gone berserk. Hurting,
he wanted so much to be *liked* at Trinity. That craving
to be popular was starved because of explosive outbursts when old tapes played from his prior congregations. He drove himself hard, self-seducing his
role into a would-be family systems pastor. But
Trinity had tasted a better way. Leadership dynamics collapsed in turmoil.

Any solid pastor risks burnout and satisfaction poverty in congregations that shove pastors into leader-ship-from-the-top positions. While this does not mean that pastors who dominate are unhealthy, I find that clergy who get their psycho-emotional energy fix from such a role often have skeletons aplenty rattling in their early biographical closets.

Is a solution, then, to concoct a mutual ministry model which slices up the Leadership pie between pastoral and lay leaders? Hardly. The effort could resemble another rearrangement of deck chairs on the Titanic. If you do not know *who* you are as a congrega-tion and who your leader is, it can turn out to be little more than rolling dice. Reconstruct your congrega-tion's *leadership* engine using the Triad model (dis-cussed in *Church Vitality*) to incorporate PEG's (Purpose Embodiment Groups, page 18) with the pastoral and laity igniters in that engine. But even that move would remain short on fuel for the engine.

We can state the matter another way: a *purposeful* bonding mechanism has characterized vital movements including churches for many centuries. When purpose ties bind or glue your congregation together, you are energized for vitality!

Time Bomb #3: More Drain than Gain

In churches like Bethany, the most gifted leaders have declined leadership positions or are performing far below their capabilities and aspirations. Why? The reasons are more systemic than personal: that congre-gation is draining off its leaders' energy.

This is a chronic scenario in family-system congregations. With a basically emotional bonding mechanism, rarely can they generate enough emotional energy to hold things together. Why? The church system exists by *volunteers* there by choice rather than by genetic or marital obligation. The energy deficiency is covered by taking from members, spending their personal emotional and spiritual capital to rescue chronic shortfalls in leadership and bonding.

Burn Out at Prince of Peace

Prince of Peace is eight years old. Like many mission starts, three to five years after getting into their new sanctuary, Prince of Peace went into a severe case of church burn out. The struggle to get started up had bonded members together like a family, they said. Their pioneering era also turned the place in on itself. This self-destructive posture, usually intensified by debt pressure, is so common in new congregations. To attach *Mission* to their status can be an absurdity.

In eight years, Prince of Peace had eight presidents. Every one resigned from the job before their terms expired. Every one of them either dropped out or quit the church. I interviewed four of these ex-leaders. Their most intense complaint was that Prince of Peace drained off most of their emotional energy. "Depleted drop outs" would accurately describe their fate.

USING THE 60/40 PRINCIPLE

I have urged congregations and other institutions to commit themselves to this principle: leaders are to *grow* personally as much as they *give* of themselves. For example, your church can move toward using the "60/

40 Principle." Averaged over a year's time, any board or council will spend no more than 60 percent of its time on business agendas, while devoting 40 percent of its time to board or council members' personal growth. Curiously enough, hard-headed business institutions have implemented the 60/40 Principle much more quickly than have churches. Some complain that it is not realistic or do-able. What is really meant, intentionally or not, is something like: "Our Church is a *Taker* rather than a *Giver.*" No wonder you are declining or plateaued, at best.

Honestly, now: what is your satisfaction wage scale? That is what you *pay* volunteers. It is also a major component in your professional workers' compensation package. Many pastors who are less than ten years away from retirement know to the month how long they have to go until retirement. In my opinion, this is another indicator of an awful fact: never has clergy vocational dissatisfaction been as pervasive and severe as it is right now. Furthermore, it seems to be even worse among clergy serving on church-wide or national denominational staffs than it is among parish pastors.

Time Bomb #4: We Have Always Done It That Way

Sameness is enormously important to family systems, including their ecclesiastical versions. That premium on sameness cripples most congregations' evangelism programs.

Bench-Sliding

I had never seen it before: inch-by-inch, members of this country congregation slid toward the center aisle during the hymn before the sermon. I asked many of them why they were doing that. "Dunno. Guess it's because we have always done it that way." Over and over again, I got the same answer.

During an interview, a 100-year old member told me this bench-sliding went back to the first building they had. There was a pot-bellied stove in the center aisle. He reminded me that sermons were much longer then and winters a lot colder. The Elders' job was to put more coal in that stove during the pre-sermon hymn. Members just slid toward it to get warmer.

I mentioned that there is no stove in the church's center aisle any more. The old man chuckled: "I know that. We have had two church buildings since then. But we have always done it that way."

Does your denomination have a new hymnal? Will your like-a-family congregation be among those most distressed by prospects of changing the service? What about evangelism? God forbid we should get anybody really *different* in here. Different skin color? Okay, just so they have the same personal priorities and aspirations we have. You want to make changes in the church office? "Remember: you are the *church* secretary, not the pastor's secretary!" Heritage or rut?

Being a preacher's kid, I spent at great deal of time at Zion Lutheran church. Those infrequent Norwegian language services seemed really weird to me. Dad disliked them a lot, and I had no idea what those sing-song noises meant. But I do remember one Epiphany service conducted for the Norwegians among us. As Dad finished reading the Christmas Gospel in the language of his childhood, behind me Helga sighed: "Oh, so good to hear it yust the way Yee-sus said it."

Heritage, yes! *Ruts,* no. For churches, the difference between rut and grave can be only a matter of inches.

How can we distinguish healthy stewardship of heritage from deadly rut infections? One way is by observed commitment to the Alpha-Omega Principle. A decision should be weighed for its probable impacts on grandchildren as much as how strongly grandparents' way of doing things is invoked at church. Living in God's name includes making our future participate in the present as much as the past does. Alpha-Omega: from the past and from the future, right now.

Invoking *either* past or future, one or the other, is the favorite tactic of tyrants. Goals which trample on tradition are false goals, guaranteed failure goals. Goals which *honor*, embody and extend the heritage are linked to Alpha-Omega.

Goals must sustain more important purposes. Heritage-goals will collapse unless they point to greater *so thats*. Evangelism collapses down to little more than recruitment. Doctrinal integrity falls into a litmus test syndrome. When getting more members or improving doctrinal literacy are not led by Christ's own overriding purposes for the church, such ventures trivialize your church. Is *what* we are going to do, *how* we will do it, and *why* going to help us accomplish Christ's overriding purposes triad of (1) embodying God's compassionate love in Christ, (2) seeking and saving the lost, and (3) preparing the world for His return?

Sameness; leadership from the top; drained do-ers; hobbled by habits: These are typical time bombs for like-a-family churches, especially when their most important priority is maintenance of family's ties.

While much can be learned from family systems theory, especially for sorting out deficient or destructive relationships and behavior, I advise using a heavy dose

of caution. I observe two underlying yet related deficiencies in these theories:
1. dismissal or heavy discounting of interactive purposes, and
2. ignoring the importance of belief systems for a vital church.

Church systems are distinct from family systems—at least, vital and healthy ones are. (See "Church Systems" in *Church Vitality*.) I keep abreast of current developments in family systems theory as one aid for sorting out where things went wrong in a troubled congregation. I want to know what seduced that church into implosion, turning in on itself, setting in motion predictable patterns of self-destruction. Those theories are helpful for analyzing and tracking the troubles, but I think they have little prescriptive worth because of those two crucial deficiencies.

Family-feeling can be a blessing, a good thing for any church. However, it becomes a curse when you let it call the shots for your congregation.

OBSTACLES TO VITALITY

If Only We Had the Right Pastor!

"How many of you have heard of St. Lorenz congregation in Frankenmuth, Michigan?" I like to ask Missouri Synod groups this question. Every hand goes up. "How many of you can tell me the name of their present Senior Pastor?" Few hands go up.

For generations, this has been an extraordinary congregation. True, St. Lorenz has been served well by some exceptional pastors. But long ago the *congregation* got its act together, avoiding the roller coaster ups-and-downs of dependence upon who the senior pastor is.

Thank God, there are such robust landmark congregations in most denominations. From generation to generation, they are *getting the job done!* Amidst recent fascination with fast-growing churches, media-touted, studied and imitated, the durable characteristics of these *landmark* congregations can be overlooked by those seeking keys to quick success for their own church.

The *quickie key* that troubled churches most often seek is the *right pastor.* Given the number of congregations buying into hyper-dependency toward clergy, the *right pastor* is in woefully short supply. It would seem that the *right pastor* is outnumbered 1,000-to-1 by the *wrong pastor* (i.e. the one we have had for too long and who is the reason *we* are not a fast-growing church).

Several experts encourage this fantasy by claiming that strong pastoral leadership is essential for a growing church. A major problem in stagnant or declining congregations is that they believe strong pastoral leadership *creates* a growing church.

Confusion over how necessary strong pastoral leadership should be probably stems from two fallacies:
1. ignoring vast differences between growth and vitality; and
2. the failure of most American denominations to develop a viable doctrine of Church and Ministry.

A bottom line result is bottom line thinking. Numbers take on exaggerated importance, and they become both decisive and definitive. *Ministry becomes Management.* Worse yet: how well a congregation does is thought to depend on *who* the pastor is.

Hyper-dependency's Coin has Two Faces—The front side of the coin of hyper-dependency is usually a short-term blessing: the presence and impact of an especially effective pastor, a pastor who has it all. But if that Pastor Tyger also *does* it all (over-functions), hyper-dependency will corrupt that church's character, particularly during its formative years. In a congregation's early history, there is so little money and so much debt, and members' initiatives have not yet taken hold of mechanics. A founding pastor has to fill many trivial gaps. The problem does not lie with an exceptionally decisive pastor. Hyper-dependency becomes a problem when Bethany's sense of *Why* or *so thats* is co-opted by or revolves around Pastor Tyger. "I cannot really tell you what our church is all about, but there goes Pastor Tyger." You become known as "Tyger's Church."

The flip side of this hyper-dependency coin is no less typical. "Everything will straighten out here once Pastor leaves." I hear this side most often in churches which did have the *right pastor* early on or at the very start of their history. If Pastor Tyger was succeeded by Pastor Pussycat, members will tell you how everything went downhill during that poor successor's tenure. But each "Tyger" among its later pastors will confide how exhausting it was to serve there, even to the point of being health-threatening.

Hyper-dependency easily happens in the church because many pastors are tempted to become indispensable, to the point of qualifying for "Key Man" insurance policies. If congregations have highly-motivated Pastor Tygers *and* an identity crisis or fuzzy Purpose System, their hyper-dependent character is set. It will have to be intentionally superceded.

SATISFACTION WAGES

Recognition usually weighs more heavily in this profession's compensation package than in higher-paying lines of work. Most churches do a terrible job in paying satisfaction wages to professional staff, with even a worse pay scale for volunteers. Like most congregations, Bethany does poorly in providing meaningful reinforcement for its volunteers' church work and for the integrity of *their* own vocational call.

Are You Paying Less than Minimum Wage?

Healthy and distressed parsonages alike sometimes reflect a frustration that their pastors may be among the most under-utilized clergy in their denomination. This feeling is most prevalent wherever both congregation and denomination ignore satisfaction wage aspects of clergy compensation. This satisfaction wage means recognition which reinforces the pastor's own sense that work being done counts for something in members' lives. It does not mean recognition that panders to ego.

How important is your satisfaction wage scale at church? I have observed a pretty consistent pattern: the more conflicted the situation, the more *dis*-satisfied the pastor and parsonage become with whatever the financial package is. In other words, avoiding Bethany's conflict-prone habits costs far too much, including the dollars Bethany will have to add on to compensate for the higher level of job dissatisfaction imposed.

Coping with Hyper-Dependency

A congregation's identity and overriding purposes must *work* and must call the shots at all levels of its fellowships and functions. It is amazing how many pastors out there can become the *right pastor* for such a purpose-led congregation! Cherish a Pastor Nauw who grafts Ordained and Called ministry into Bethany's root system, rather than coming in like a potted plant deposited briefly on your church's doorstep.

Ever since the apostolic church, our tradition of the priesthood of believers is depicted by this imagery of a common root system for mutual ministry. The biblical model of vine-and-branches assumes the same root-stock with distinct branches grafted into the same vine, each bearing fruit. Remember: It is *branches* which bear fruit, not twigs or solitary God-and-Me leaves that wither and fall off after a short season.

Pastors need to remember that leaders who do not *know* their members are not *followed*. Remember the Shepherd: "I know my sheep and they know my voice." Know your members and the congregation's heritage, its *persona* as a body, its distinctive church systems. For example, this means you do not mess around with the chancel or sanctuary set-up until you know *why* they had this arrangement before you got there. Before you even think about moving the font, read its memorial plaque name and find out about it. Profaning the dead is a far more serious transgression in peoples' minds than is being out of step with the latest liturgical fads. Basic theological principles filter which "neat ideas" you place into use.

With the advent of mass higher education, pastors are no longer the best educated people in town. This development is still ignored in most denominations' doctrines of Church and Ministry. The biblical model of "Shepherd" cannot justify an autocratic or control-obsessed style of ministry.

The laity need to know that the shepherd species is distinct from the flock. A shepherd is much more than just a full-time professional sheep, and also something well beyond a manager. The distinction resides in the

Office of ministry, not in the *person* in that Office. While the Office of ordained and called ministry is essential to Bethany and a major definitive component in its self-understanding, the personal qualities and views of Pastor Nauw are *not*.

One question that Bethany's members need to ask themselves is: do they have a clear sense of where they have to support that Office, and where they can disagree, even strongly, with the pastor's personal opinions?

Congregations that get hung up on getting the *right pastor* are typically blind to the Body. Are you a grab-bag of spiritual soloists or the living *Body* of Christ at your time and place? Discern and keep revealing the One New Person which God has created for your congregation: the living Body of Christ, the bigger than all of us dimension of a true Christian church. The Body is a living *dimension*, not a separate coterie of true-blue believers who just happen to be "on our side."

Through troubles and his deliberate deceits, Satan tries to conceal this living dimension from us. He encourages our preoccupation with organizational management matters and institutional self-interest to divert us from the things most needful.

"Why should we care about our congregation?"

This is a good rallying question for every board and group at Bethany. *Why?* Unless Bethany has its purposeful act together, it will be on roller-coaster rides of hyper-dependency on whomever its pastoral and lay leadership happen to be.

Family systems congregations do a real number on *any* leadership, clergy or laity. Such churches are parasites, leeching the emotional and spiritual resources from their leadership.

Leaders at Bethany drop out of office once their term is up, if they last that long. Emotionally bonded, rather than *purpose* bonded, family systems churches are incapable of generating enough emotional energy on their own. So, they have to drain others; typical victims are those leaders whom the *system* entices onto eldest child pedestals.

Afterword

As analytic tool, family systems theory can be helpful for sorting out congregational dysfunction. As a prescriptive approach for troubled churches, however, it is profoundly flawed. Belief has no key role in Family Systems theory, and its emotional bonding emphasis just does not mix with that purpose bonding which historically characterizes vital ideological groups and movements. Indeed, the more "like a family" a congregation becomes, the deeper the hole it digs for itself. Such places leave healthy pastors and lay leaders spiritually and emotionally and even physically burned out.

Getting out of that hole does not happen over night, but it can be done. How to change your small groups from their activity or "affinity-based" character into PEG's (Purpose Embodiment Groups), how to reconstruct your church's leadership system, how to shift toward an outsurge posture: these are ingredients for a strategy to move from plateaus to church vitality.

10

Codependency Cliques

Among the most polarized congregations with which
I have worked, at least two-thirds have been distorted by codependency networks. In each instance,
members were unwittingly drawn into a codependent
clique. When pastors were involved, most were unaware of how it happened.

There is an abundance of codependency gibberish in
today's literature. Some of it is realistic, some services
New Age narcissism. My first-hand experience involves how codependency cliques impact local congregations.

*What are these networks or cliques, and why can a
congregation be so tormented by them?*

According to health sciences research, codependency
usually originates from childhood traumas. Adult survivors may have had alcoholic parents or grandparents.
They may be survivors of childhood sexual or physical
abuse. Many of these adult COA's or survivors are
motivated to enter the helping professions. Some stud-

ies estimate nearly thirty percent of ministers, professionals in social work, counseling and medicine have
emerged from these childhood traumas. This should
not imply, however, that this is the *main* reason they
enter these professions. Clergy who are *acknowledged*
ACOA's and have come to grips with their past are some
of the most effective pastors I know.

Reluctant Ministries

When pastors, staff members or lay leaderships have
difficulty working with early adolescents or pre-teens,
this should encourage a closer look by them and by you
at the *why*. Examine *why* Pastor Withit has trouble
working redemptively with this age group, trouble
teaching and relating to them on *gospel* wave lengths,
trouble interpreting its healing power through personal
biographical examples from those same years.

Late childhood and early adolescence may have
been the most spiritually and emotionally distressed
time in an ACOA or adult survivor's life. This is a time
when personal experience of the Gospel is crushed
under massive family relationship burdens which
multiply the Law's weight, already heavy enough during teenage years. In later years, memory of some
pastors' own Confirmation-age trauma *still* has not been
healed and still is trapped in bondage to the Law.

How can Pastor Withit teach and exemplify God's
love, grace and forgiveness in Christ with adolescents?
They are in that stage of life which is still filled with so
many minefields in his own memory. Often such pastors and Christian workers will either openly scorn their
work with Confirmation-age youngsters or noticeably
under-function in this area of ministry.

There may be other factors at work, but these also may be associated with old guilts. Areas of notable reluctance or under-functioning that contrast with solid performance in other phases of ministry should be a flag to look beneath surface appearances.

Beyond the array of codependency markers, this one has special relevance for church professionals: how does Pastor Withit use personal childhood or early teen years credible experiences in sermons and teaching? It is typical for members to be uninformed about abusive-childhood pastors' pre-16 biography. One further corollary of this: I notice such church workers usually march in the ranks of the humor-impaired.

It is not difficult to pick up the trail left by COA's/Survivors in church systems. Ministry is, after all, so contextual. The markers are especially tough to camouflage in congregations whose own bonding mechanisms are defective, e.g. when they resemble family systems.

Barry

Pastor Anton's best friend was Barry, a skilled and experienced parish pastor with CPE (Clinical Pastoral Education) Supervisor status. A partner Audicator with me throughout this consultation, Barry also had been helping Anton sort out some residues from his mother's family system.

But Pastor Anton left a trail in the congregation that pointed to him being a COA. Anton never saw his late father touch a drink. "But the trail is here!" I told Barry, then Anton. Pressed several times over several hours, Anton's jaw suddenly dropped. "There was this one time when I was small. Dad had a glass of wine. He almost fell down." His Dad was a dry alcoholic; the small drink triggered a neuro-physical overload remaining from years before. The pieces finally began to fit together. By its contextual nature, the Conflict Redemption process may pick up important factors sometimes beyond the reach of strictly clinical apparatus.

In my experience, few ACOA's and adult survivors seek *treatment* at church. Most are ready and capable of developing their own supports and means of healing. Most ACOA's have no worse a biography than the rest of the membership. When they are not networked, these fellow Christians are an integral resource to a congregation's outsurging mission and vitality. We all breathe the same redemptive atmosphere of a church which purposefully emphasizes reliance on how our doctrine works for daily dying and rising in Christ, for healing and vitality.

In childhood, these victims learn skills and acquire attitudes which enable them to survive and to make the best of a terrifying situation. For example, the eldest child of an alcoholic often is forced into heavy responsibilities in a household where one or more of the adults are frequently dysfunctional or abusive. Younger children may feel less responsibility but share acquired skills such as "lying" to protect their parent(s). They may invent a non-existent achievement to enhance a parent's reputation. Many of us want our parents to be perceived as more successful than they actually are. But the ACOA or adult survivors are more desperate about it.

In adulthood, their compensatory impulse comes off as lying. The difference between what they *wish* had happened and what actually did occur gets fuzzy. This typical survival skill is learned in late childhood or early adolescence to cover for traumatizing household episodes.

Research evidence is still fragmentary and incomplete on this widespread phenomenon. For example, we still are not clear on what role a child's birth-order plays in the scheme of things. Read three researchers on this subject and at least three opposite findings emerge. As are most new psycho-emotional discoveries, this one's explanatory worth for most of us can be grossly exaggerated.

Why is this relevant for congregations?

Its relevancy lies in the vulnerability of adult survivors to *network* or bond with others having similar childhood traumas. Remarkably, some will bond even prior to mentioning their common experience. The network or bonded group can become intense, exceeding merits of surface or apparent commonalties. When you find yourself wondering what clique members see in each other, red flags should go up.

I believe such codependency networking appears in churches because of participants' redemptive expectations of their congregation. These expectations may include release from lingering guilt over "What did I do to cause Mom (or Dad or Uncle) to do this to me?" There is nothing wrong with this hope. But it can be devastating when churches ignore it, refuse to understand it, or refrain from turning this experience to productive ministries through the Body of Christ!

Why is this of concern to **your** church?

Because a codependency clique usually severely distorts the Body of Christ's bonding integrity. Spiritually and psycho-emotionally, it is a false tie that binds.

Codependency Cliques Develop:

INFORMAL RADAR

We Norwegians seem to be able to spot each other from a sea of Germans or Swedes at church conventions. Maybe this ethnic radar resembles the way codependency cliques start. If we ignore the bonding glue of these cliques, their fellowship can becoming extremely destructive.

The Refugees

It actually happened: a group of women were exceptionally effective in their church's work with overseas refugees. While they were heartfelt Christians, at least two troublesome ties bonded them: (1) they were vehemently anti-pastor, and (2) they concluded their twice-monthly home Bible study group meetings by drinking themselves into near-stupor! Their clique started informally.

They were better informed biblically and doctrinally than most members. But their tactics at board and congregational meetings came to fit each of the two favored strategies of codependency cliques: Mongooses, darting in and back quickly to mortally assault their intended victim on the aisle's other side; or, as would-be Pirates who mount a frontal campaign to take control of the church vessel. Yet, rarely have I interviewed members who cared more passionately about their congregation's spiritual integrity and single-minded mission than these women. Fortunately for them and their congregation, Pastor Lowell knew and cared about their false ties that bind.

CRISIS COINCIDENCE

Crisis coincidence is probably the most common vehicle for a pastor's involvement within a congregational codependency network, *if* that pastor is either an *unacknowledged* adult COA or an adult survivor.

Any pastor's top priority has to be effective response to members' personal crisis, whether death, serious accident, job loss, divorce. Pastors must drop less important stuff in order to render effective and timely pastoral Christ-Care. So far, so good. The problem arises when a pastor allows or encourages recipients' appreciation of Christ-Care to deteriorate into *dependence* on the pastor! I believe pastors rarely make a deliberate attempt to encourage this to happen. But if a pastor's own survivor experience has never been dealt with, watch out! Remember: *Unacknowledged* COA's or adult survivors are problematic for congregations, not *acknowledged* COA's.

Pastor Pete's Problem

Hope's former Pastor Pete had affairs with several women members. He had formed such a powerful codependency network among members that when I arrived for a Consultation years after he had been "de-frocked," network members said to me: "We know Pastor was committing adultery. Outrageously so, too. But look at all the good he was doing for God's Kingdom in the meantime." I kid you not! Every member of his still-lingering network had been drawn into it after their pastor had given timely and quality caring during members' intense personal crisis. In their eyes, Pastor Pete's successor could do nothing right. Of course not!

NINE MARKERS OF CODEPENDENCY NETWORKS IN CHURCH SYSTEMS

1. Adamant loyalty to an individual

One marker of codependency cliques is adamant loyalty given to a pastor, church secretary, organist or other leader at your church—if this loyalty obviously exceeds the merits of that person's achievements.

As the network accumulates characteristics of an extended family, one is tempted to think of it as a cult. Despite superficial parallels, it probably lacks key qualifications for a cult. For instance, cult members typically are low-achieving children from high-achieving "successful" families. Whatever the cult *believes* has little to do with why people join it. They are drawn to a "Family System" the Guru has created, a loyal family its recruits perceive they never had. They are led to believe they will achieve more through this cult family than they could ever accomplish in their family-of-origin.

2. Excusing immorality or malfeasance

Recall Pastor Pete's many adulteries and his clique members' excusing of them. Clique members will overlook a church leader's obvious malfeasance in other areas of responsibility, his or her addictive behaviors, and even rudeness. This is true when the pastor camouflages their relationship with the cloak of evangelism or another noble cause.

Rolling the Dice

In one congregation plagued with codependency networks, their pastor habitually disappeared for two or three days after each church council or congregational meeting. This fellow ran off for a binge at a nearby racetrack. Why? As an adult, the COA sometimes opts for an addiction different from the parent's. Back at church, this pastor was dysfunctional much of the time. In covering for him, his codependency clique wrapped themselves in the flag of quarreling about how much money the congregation was designating for its school.

3. Compulsive "Kingdom Work"

Compulsive busyness is said to identify a Type A personality. But such compulsiveness can stem from acquired childhood avoidance techniques such as avoiding the chaos created by an inebriated parent. This can result in a compulsion to help people outside their family in a more effective manner than the child was able to help at home.

The Reverend Rushover

Reverend Rushover, a retired pastor, was contracted by First Church to go calling two days a week. Over those years he was under contract, three excellent senior pastors were driven out by a faction supportive of Pastor Rushover. Just a few hours into my consultation, red flags went up when I heard that Pastor Rushover called six days a week instead of the agreed-upon two days. Instead of 20 calls, he made closer to 60 calls per week. If someone was hospitalized, Pastor Rushover hurried so he could get there before the senior pastor.

"See how dedicated he still is to Kingdom Work," his clique said. Others risked suspicion of opposing God's way when they questioned Pastor Rushover and his clique's actions within the congregation. From childhood, Pastor Rushover's traveling salesman father beat him viciously each time he returned from a trip.

Some of us are "Type A" personalities, like those pastors who have their sermons done by *Monday*. Others are driven to hard work by thoroughly admirable motives. But we do not form gangs who camouflage their real identity with church work. Constituting a red flag is the combination of the leader's compulsive hard work and a "faction" made up of clones (of that leader).

4. Overreactions

Frequent overreactions to situations usually signal that an *individual's* past is running amok or deflected distress is involved. These overreactions can indicate a closer look is needed, especially if other markers are present.

In one instance, inquiry about a *group's* members suggested that the only common thread tying them together was the probability of a codependency. They were so dissimilar in other respects: type of jobs, income levels, church background, ethnographically, personality styles. But they shared a crucial experience: abused childhoods. Their "mongoose" effect on the church's decision-making and spirit was devastating.

5. Excessive demands to be heard

Andy's Demands

Andy, the music director, was our final interview on that consultation day. Andy demanded twice as much time as everyone else's 45-minute interview. At the closure session two days later, Andy was furious because he could not give yet another speech. In their follow-up work, Audicators were badgered by Andy with his ever-present dossier of grievances. When he was not doing the complaining, five of his close allies were.

Just because a member is outspoken at meetings does not flag possible codependency. The flag comes up when he or she is speaking for a clearly marked group (who may, in fact, be writing much of the speaker's script). Look for characteristics of this group's use of language:

a) similarity of jargon (a typical in-group glue) which means far more to the group than to others;

b) visible disparity between language and behavior, especially in the relatively higher importance assigned to language. (Theories vary on childhood origins for this reliance on verbal weapons.)

c) Gospel substance and spirit are not in their vocabulary.

6. Compulsive nagging about youth ministries

Demands for the congregation to devote an excessive portion of its resources for ministry to one's own children may signal a distinctive variation in the transgenerational pattern of COA/adult survivors.

Abusive behavior is often passed on from generation to generation, unless intentional effort is given to breaking that pattern. Josh, an abusive church leader, was abused as a child. He demanded a miraculous ministry for his own children from a church his children despise.

This pattern seems to be: a family's present generation may embrace an active church life which the grandparent(s) avoided. But the next generation rejects it.

7. Camouflaging symbol

Diverse aspects of any congregation's ministry usually have their champions, supportive allies and advocates who carry the ball for that ministry sector. But red flags should go up when people barricade that sector as a symbol which could be camouflaging their churchly alliances. The symbol may be some on-going project, pre-school, a cause, program, a style of evangelism, parochial school, music, issues such as communion practices or the role of women. Closer consideration of this group's possible codependency should be flagged by:

- *Aggressive negativism* toward competing congregational ministry sectors, often coupled with noticeably withheld support or encouragement for those sectors.

- *Prolonged polarization* over their symbol is kept fueled largely by this group. Bethany was *not* governed by clear overriding purposes that would keep this group's symbol in proper perspective. Polarization is intensified by a church's Purpose System collapse as much as by these people's deliberate actions.

- *Power base maintenance:* Not all who vote with the group in support of its symbol are codependents. But the group will solicit occasional allies for those crucial decisions which result in maintaining enough power to keep the symbol barricaded.

Though usually unnoticed by outsiders, the group periodically creates loyalty test episodes. These take place when the symbol is run up a flagpole to check on who salutes it *and* to condemn those who do not.

8. Non-transferable loyalty

When crisis ministry recipients remain loyal only to caregiver(s) without entering into the congregation's mainstream fellowship and functions, look closely at the prospect of codependency with those caregivers or a support group.

Upon departure of the group's originating caregiving hero, who may be different from its official leader, three traits may surface:

a) The group inflates their hero's merits and achievements to the farthest limits that can be verified by the church's memory.

b) Next, the group attempts to co-opt that hero's memory to legitimize their position, as though they were the truest heirs of the hero's heritage.

c) "We need a *strong Leader!*" This refrain is a red flag if other indications of codependency are apparent, especially when this insistent refrain overrides clear evidence the congregation needs to get *its own* act together. The statement may be meant to indict an incumbent pastor, or it may be used as an attempt to co-opt a vacancy period or calling process.

9. Obsession with control

Obsession with control is probably the most common and disruptive of all these markers. Harry grew up in a household that kept going out of control, so his childhood survival skills responded to a desperate agenda: "How can I get this catastrophe under control?" The strategies Harry worked out served a singular purpose: to restore some semblance of stability. *Now,* however, those childhood survival skills keep predisposing his posture toward everyday uncertainties and relationships, including those at church. Whatever the issue, transaction or relationship might be, it becomes another challenge to his disposition toward control.

Although it was not Harry's intent, results from his control ploys sorely wounded the Body of Christ. Harry kept sliding into those lifelong control agendas when something happened that flicked a switch and old tapes started playing.

Are the outcomes entirely his fault? No! Members' control impulses are most likely to be activated whenever the congregation bogs down in its collapsed Purpose System. As long as a church is functioning no higher than the lower two purpose levels, it provides ideal growing conditions for control vines to bear bumper crops.

Presence of several markers does not *prove* that a person or that group is codependent. These symptomatic markers are listed so that Christ-caregiving ministry can move into place for those in need.

Two Types of Church Codependency Cliques

CLERGY

The most *noticeable* type of codependency clique revolves around a pastor or other full-time professional church worker. Remember that care recipients' appreciation for crisis ministry can get turned into codependency if all parties are not conscious of what can happen. I repeat that this transition from appreciation to codependency rarely is deliberate on anyone's part. But where there is a *vivid polarization* between groups (particularly over a pastor), at least one codependency clique is likely to be complicating things.

POWER BLOCS

The most common type of cliques are power blocs that remain bonded regardless of what is being debated or decided. Lillian is part of such a bloc. Despite her *personal* better judgment on a given matter, she is continually co-opted by the bloc leader's views. That leader's voice may never be heard at a congregational or board meeting. He or she is the script writer, the Grey Eminence behind what others in the bloc say out loud.

When ordinary cliques have several obvious reasons for bonding, such as long-time friendship, similarities in outside interests, children in the same age bracket, or personality attractions, they are socialized cliques rather than codependency networks. But when their affinities just do not make sense, look beneath the surface for possible codependency.

On the other hand...

I have *never* encountered a troubled congregation where it could be said that codependent cliques were either the root or center of that church's problems. The more dysfunctional a church system, the more vulnerable it is to disruption by such groups. They may add fuel to the fire, but they did not light it. Rather than dump blame on them, it is far more important and productive for the congregation to regard such networks as an opportunity for Christ-Care.

Few of your COA / adult survivor members are networked, and most have not been co-opted by an active clique. Their expectations and roles in church ministry are at least as Christ-centered and altruistic as those of other active members.

It does not follow that because people have this tragic biographical component, they will be trouble for a church. Most can and will do worthwhile ministries and will have invaluable insights to share.

Coping with Codependency Cliques

Persecution, attack or shaming-strategies will further entrench and solidify a clique and trigger survival skills developed during childhood. Most members of a *disruptive* codependency clique are active in church precisely because it is the most redemptive possibility available to them. Nevertheless, the Body of Christ's integrity and vitality must be attended to.

1. De-authorize the clique.

Any and all *negative* codependency cliques in a congregation must be de-authorized. If the group is actually wounding the Body of Christ, efforts to cut them off from their audience may be in order. Why is this your strategic key? What techniques can a pastor use to cut them off from their audience?

Some historical perspective may be helpful. Once a dissenting movement was cut off from its audience, it turned in on itself, increasing loyalty pressures on its own constituency until it *self*-destructed. This happened to every heresy in church history. Orthodoxy rarely, if ever, defeated those movements. Instead, they *self*-destructed. The only hard-ball strategies that worked at all were those focused upon turning a movement in on itself, to accelerate that self-destructive process.

For example:

Historically, the Mainstreams tried to have dissenters regarded as mad or as profoundly immoral. Who will listen to a madman? Who wants to support immorality? Even today, the Soviets are less likely to put dissenters on trial than to commit them for psychiatric treatment, or for prolonged residence in a mental hospital. It cuts off dissenters from an audience and expanding their constituency.

During fourth-century doctrinal battles over Christology and the Trinity, the immorality option was expertly practiced by major factions in the Athanasian side against the Arian heretics. Either hardball option takes much more skill than most of us have to use for *productive* outcomes. A gentler form of this ancient tactic is to brand the other conflictor(s) as in need of counseling. These options will more often backfire on those who venture them.

Warning!

Beware of taking any slanderous course of action, no matter how furious and frustrated you have become. If your underlying motive is to conquer or get rid of the groups rather than open up *redemptive* moves, you are likely to blow it. You may even end up with a lawsuit on your hands.

Therefore, the course I have followed in these situations is to set in motion a two-stage sequence:

a) Deprive the group(s) of their audience among non-group members of the congregation, *in order* to

b) Set the stage for redemptive ministries to each person in that network.

1) The Board or Council should consult on this. "There is evidence that what the health sciences call codependency cliques are present in our congregation." Explain and discuss. Do not get embroiled in proving a case. Expect close inquiry as to the statement's accuracy *and* integrity.

But do not go even this far unless the next step is forthcoming.

2) Agree on and commit to a specific comprehensive Christ-Care ministry to any and each member of such a clique, including who does what, when, how. "We have been *reacting* rather than *responding* to some real hurts and needs."

2. Carry out Christ-Care ministries to those within the clique(s).

Often, an adult COA or adult survivor is burdened with enormous guilt. They need supportive relationships with others who know what it is like. These cliques bond so closely. They become a problem to the church when the group's long-time control skills are galvanized and driven by guilt projections. Normal associations and alliances elsewhere in the congregation are no match for these ecclesiastical guerillas.

Some clique participants see the network as their safeguard against personal disintegration. Exercise Spirit-led care so they are not robbed of this crutch without having an actively redemptive alternative available. Such well-meant robbery could trigger self-destructive processes for one or more clique members.

I have seen codependency cliques change quickly into healthier and productive support groups when they are re-oriented around Christ-Care. Directed beyond themselves and beyond the group's internal support myopia, they can become remarkably capable of switching off self-destructive currents and developing new circuits for members' interaction. However, if your congregation's priorities are bogged down in institutional self-interest or the congregational *system* lags behind that group's new Christ-Care commitment, the codependency clique's leader obtains even greater authorization than before.

To put it bluntly: If your church's systems are functionally bonded around false or inferior *purpose,* little can be done about these cliques until Bethany gets its act together! (See *Church Vitality,* "Church Systems" chapter)

But if Bethany is getting its act together, a Board or the Council may also consider specific recourse to the Five Steps resource of Matthew 18.

    a) Are there helps available through the church (including through your regional jurisdiction) which might *supplement*, not *replace*, the congregation's efforts with these codependents at Step Three?

    b) Are there possibilities of Steps Regression, of providing use of Step Two for each codependent if his or her parent(s) may be available?

    c) When would their use of one of the Bond of Peace services be appropriate, timely, a blessing?

Codependency cliques are more common in Christian congregations than we suspected. At your church, they may not be notably disruptive, especially if the congregation is growing and if many people are participating in activities. Codependents may not be as apparent or disruptive in more expansive contexts as they usually are in plateaued or declining churches.

If your congregation's systems are circuited around clearly redemptive, outsurging overriding purposes, you are already positioned for authentic ministry to these people. Very likely you will find them welcoming it!

Afterword

Codependency has crossed fad-land's border in America, although hard research data remains scarce. This chapter is not about people's everyday codependent relationships, but about how this phenomenon can distort and disrupt a congregation. I describe what I have seen, intending this as an introduction rather than The Final Word. One point cannot be over-emphasized:

avoid shoot-from-the-hip "diagnosis"! The nine markers add up to an *alert* rather than a guarantee. Just as
some people display characteristics of an ACOA or
adult survivor but did not, in fact, come from abusive
homes, similar superficial coincidences may apply to a
group of "mongooses" at your church.

The good news is that codependent networks are
dealt with more readily in churches than in most other
contexts. More easily camouflaged, too, however, typically wrapping themselves in Holy War or Noble Cause
flags.

11

Notes from the Underground

———————— ▭ ————————

Some very private dysfunctions can weave their way into a congregation's fabric. Some of the threads are pulled from tattered personal biographies; more come from recent everyday troubles.

Power Sharks

Power Sharks stick out like sore thumbs on the Body of Christ. How rarely they realize three sad facts of church life:

- Their ways are as transparent as a sheet of mylar,
- How little respect other members have for them,
- How much their control agendas reveal an unhealthy biography.

Until quite recently, they got away with it. But now as more and more church members are seeing correlations between what goes on "outside" and what is happening in their troubled congregations, the ground under power sharks gets shakier.

"I saw it on Oprah."   Others regarded this interviewee as one of their sweet little old lady members,
active and hard-working, but hardly in their leader
ranks. She described what she had seen on other day-
time talk shows. "Well, the way Mr. St. George acts at
Voters, I'll bet he is one of them. You know, from an
abused childhood. Only he is taking it out on our
church." Pop psychology, no doubt, but with more than
a few grains of truth to it, as it turned out in that case.

"There is an Old Guard that has been throwing its
weight around here for as long as anybody remembers."
Several months ago I heard this complaint from the
president of a four-year-old mission congregation. How
could that be? "Well, they were of the Old Guard in their
former congregations." Maybe this was a case of mov-
able birthright.

Some church members cannot resist trying to control
any group they join. The idealistic theory is that they
should be diverted into groups and given responsibilities that are peripheral rather than essential. By all
means, to keep them off the church council! Nice theory,
but it rarely works. I can think of at least three options:

1. Expect a miracle. A bolt of lightning from God's
   hand strikes them and behold: a miraculous
   change of personality!
2. Fight power with power. MAD (Mutually Assured Destruction) may be the best possible outcome from this course. Or,
3. *Dilute* their influence.

If these first two options are improbable, the third
seems as mysterious as it is sensible. Sensible because
every one of the troubled congregations with which I
have worked had become sitting ducks, paddling in
circles *long* before they became conflict-dysfunctional.

The control addict can more easily control a sitting duck congregation than a bird in flight. How so? Bethany had either lost or never had decisive overriding purposes which kept it in an *outsurging* posture. When organizational self-interest, maintenance attitudes, data-driven (bricks-budget-and-body-count) numbers tyrannize congregational choices: *there* is the ball park for control games.

In a word: Power Sharks thrive on Bethany's collapsed Purpose System.

There are ways to infiltrate skilled New Member Rookies into the starting line-up, if you like those games. Pulling this off takes a mix of skill and miracle few of us are blessed with, however. A more productive option is to build a better ball park, where control games do not play well. How?

By claiming overriding purposes that power players cannot attack without destroying their own credibility. Then, put legs on those purposes. Finally get up steam and keep moving under the authority of those clear and shared purposes.

The "Classic Purpose System" section of *Church Vitality* describes much more comprehensive strategies than I discussed in Chapter 1. In the meantime, several corollaries for a venerable principle can be noted.

Master the Heritage!

Whoever are the truest Sons and Daughters of Bethany's conscious heritage will validate whether any change is a credible and supportable expression of that heritage. "But we have never done it that way here," becomes an effective roadblock if—

1. the issue is a minor operational change validated only by personal preferences rather than by clearly more important priorities; and

2. the agents of change are ignorant of any superior tradition within that heritage.

I am continually impressed by how often the *grand-parents* of an archaic Old Guard exercised extraordinary vision and risk-taking in their church leadership roles. They were oriented toward outsurge beyond their congregation, which contrasts 180 degrees from what their current Old Guard descendants would have you believe.

Barely out of seminary, one new pastor immersed himself in old Minutes and old stories. This enabled the pastor to go privately to a Council member suffering from ecclesiastical senility at the ripe old age of 43 and gently remind her: "What would your Grandpa have done? Remember how he led the way in starting the Sunday School mission over at St. Paul's (in a neighboring town)? He did so despite opposition and sniping from those other two families in the congregation."

It is surprising how easily Old Guards can radically revise a congregation's original heritage with the net effect of turning their church in on itself. Their control-focused editing often mandates strategic revision by those who appreciate how powerful an instrument mastery of history can be for getting a church back on track and moving ahead.

The heritage has dimensions beyond any single congregation, regardless of denominational polity. Even the mega-churches are not islands unto themselves. Whether by a "Heroes of Faith" theme in Sunday School materials or serendipitous networking with the like-minded, a larger dimension of the heritage and historical accountability can be brought to bear on Bethany. Only those who are familiar with *both* local and larger dimensions of the heritage can show other members how to build the bridges.

Another corollary accents language and terminology. Throughout history, successful revolutions have used venerable thought-categories and terminology which have a credible history within the system targeted for change. They *clothed* themselves in that language. Clothe needed changes with the language of faith. If you feel uncomfortable doing so, take a hard look at your agenda's actual purposes. The effort may be difficult, but it is worthwhile because, when harmonized with Bethany's founding vision and the larger mainstream of believers, progress and improvements are more likely to be carefully worked through before being ventured. And, they will gain much broader support.

An all too common violation of the heritage principle happens during the Call process, via what may be called the "New Program Fallacy." While newer members crave a candidate's "new ideas," Old Guarders are filtering any ideas through two other criteria.

1. Is there any connection between these ideas and what we are comfortable with? And,

2. can we *control* this hotshot?

Since Bethany's decisive heritage is a family secret, candidates and Call committees do better to explore the candidate's priorities and Purpose System for ministry. They need to consider the experience and skills by which this pastor can put legs on those priorities. Do not encourage the fantasy that you are a willing market for pre-packaged programs. You could end up with a wind-up Drummer Boy toy rather than a Shepherd.

Counter-Indicators: More Than Medicinal Matters

One or more groups or systems in Bethany are notably disabled by individuals who manifest what I call "counter-indicators" to Conflict Redemption. These are warning signals that mental illness or other grave psycho-emotional disturbances may be at work and could require expert treatment.

Rather than rehashing standard symptomologies cited by health science specialists, only four of the most common counter-indicators which surface in church-systems are described here. These counter-indictors are red flags signaling that an element may be present which tells you to go easy on (or even suspend) Conflict Redemption procedures with this person until professional help can be brought to bear on the situation.

- **Compulsive Scapegoating**
- **Malice**
- **Clutching the Conflict**
- **Rejecting Responsibility**

COMPULSIVE SCAPEGOATING

All of us have done our share of scapegoating now and then. Our childish "Bobby *made* me do it, Mommmeeee" dodges rarely dissuaded grown-ups, but even as adults we sometimes do not feel up to accepting responsibility for something we have done or been party to.

We may be emotionally saturated, or we may be going through times that have us feeling particularly insecure. Recourse to the standard array of avoidance mechanisms can entice us into occasional scapegoating. Ordinarily, that will pass and we grow up a bit more. I am referring here to *compulsive* scapegoating, not its occasional appearance.

Compulsive scapegoating means refusing to accept personal responsibility for the mess you have created, either by yourself or as an accomplice. Episode after episode, time after time, confronted with clear responsibility for something that has gone wrong, the compulsive "scapegoater" blames someone else.

Oliver, a member of Bethany, deflects responsibility quite creatively. He either impugns the integrity and expertise of the person who identified Oliver's responsibility for the situation, or he accentuates his own inadequacies relative to that identifier's. ("I do not have your fancy education. I do not have any control over the matter," etc.) Of course, he shirks responsibility throughout his personal life as well as at church.

Oliver faults Donald, believing he is clearly right and that Donald's behavior or position is obviously wrong. Oliver piles on ulterior motives for Donald's behavior. "He is doing that for political reasons, to get more power," he says. When Oliver implies that Donald's intent and motives are *evil*, Oliver edges toward the borders of compulsive scapegoating where his own buried guilts are linked.

At least two forces drive this "Counter-Indicator"

One is fairly obvious: instead of claiming a troubled situation as an occasion for a healing experience, Oliver will work diligently and creatively to keep the situation non-redemptive and to isolate it from any prospect for healing. He is one of Bethany's inveterate peace-breakers.

Another underlying generator of the compulsive scapegoat artist is a destructive burden of *guilt*. Guilt permeates Oliver's being and atmosphere. It is as though he inhales and breathes the very air of guilt. This guilt has been clutched for so long it has finally taken control, almost to the point of his embracing it.

There is much scholarly speculation about how this embrace originates, how a specialist should work back from its present complexity and power. Our concern here is the realization that compulsive scapegoating can signal the presence of an emotional disturbance so severe that even the best-intentioned Conflict Redemption efforts must not tamper with it.

Oliver's mere survival may be held together by guilt, removable only in the careful process of replacing corrupt emotional-and-relationship circuitry with a healthier system. Otherwise, he could come tragically unglued. Do *not* attempt the amateur psychiatrist game with such folks.

MALICE

Malice is distinct from anger, both biblically and psychologically. Malice is a deliberate strategy for ill-effect toward others, to *make* bad things happen to them. It is quite different from ordinary displacement, projection or other avoidance mechanisms. The malicious person is purposefully trying to do you in!

Curt said, "I am going to make sure that Pastor is thrown out of the ministry." Or, "I will see to it that Pastor's next congregation hears the full story."

Such statements *may* reflect a genuine concern for other Christians and congregations, but Curt's strategy exceeds any known merits of the conflicted situation. Beware of Curt's behavior if it persists, especially after the target of his malice is demonstrating real repentance (if wrongdoing had, in fact, occurred).

As with scapegoating, Curt's malice expresses a powerful, destructive guilt. Outside of church systems, Curt would probably express it through something like virulent racism.

We all have had moments when we wished something would happen to a particular person in a way that meant we would get even. Though such ill-wishes are not nice, they are hardly sick. Here I am referring here to a virtual *posture* of malice, malicious intent as a habitual and compulsive pattern. For example, Curt was curious about *Peace in the Parish* and Conflict Redemption systems *until* he discovered they would not serve his compulsion to get even.

CLUTCHING THE CONFLICT

There are people who use visible conflict as a crutch for hidden dysfunction. Some people pick fights and soon walk away as if nothing happened. However, take careful notice of folks who refuse to let go of a conflict, even when their apparent needs have been met.

Of course, there are situations where the problem may be no more serious than an inflated sense of entitlement, of what they deserve. "I have not gotten out of this what I deserve." Felt needs remain unduly inflated, particularly when too many suns have gone down on one's anger. (See Intensive Audication in Step Two of Matthew 18:15-20 on page 77.)

Holding on to a conflict can be a grave matter for another type of person, however. Amy *needs* this conflict, clutches onto it, nurtures and prods it in order to survive. Continually over-reacting to her stated issues, Amy keeps coming back to them. It is as though she is deaf to what has just been said. Whatever issues or felt needs are on the table amount to deceptions for her, in both the biblical and psychological senses of that term.

Unless both Amy and you are equipped and willing to proceed together with intensive work on whatever underlies this clutching of a conflict, *do not* take this conflict away from her. Adamant resistance or refusal to let go of a conflict which *seems* to have been dealt with should be a clear signal something is seriously wrong beneath surface appearances or presenting issues.

Do not be dissuaded or dismayed by Amy's current resistance to expert assistance. Acceptance may happen when she gains confidence in whatever person or process offers light at the end of her dark tunnel. In the meantime, encourage and support her personal healing by getting several fellow saints into position so that she is not going it alone.

REJECTING RESPONSIBILITY

On the surface, immobilization and rejected responsibility can look alike. How might you distinguish them? Rejecting responsibility for what has to happen leads to statements like: "I have made my peace with God on this, so I do not have to deal with you anymore!" As soon as Jerry makes this statement, we can see that he is involved in one of the oldest shell games. In marriage conflict, for example, this statement all but announces that Jerry has another lover in the closet. In other conflict situations, variations on this theme usually signal a hidden agenda.

Even though there has been a breakthrough in their Conflict Redemption efforts, Jerry and Melinda may become temporarily immobilized from emotional exhaustion and claim, "We just cannot do anything more right now." Their confidence may be shaken, but you do not detect a refusal to move on with restoring their relationship. If there is a deliberate refusal to continue good-faith Conflict Redemption efforts when a breakthrough solution is imminent or has materialized, this counter-indicator demands a closer look at what is *really* going on here. Be alert when you see:

1. Active, deliberate shunning or dismissing a conflicted relationship,
2. Refusing to continue good-faith Conflict Redemption efforts when a breakthrough solution is imminent or has actually materialized.

A suggestion: One way to discern whether these are counter-indicators or just a short-term immobility is to venture conversation about the God-created One New Person relationship which is at stake. How do these conflictors react? Does either Jerry or Melinda refuse to budge from an autonomous ego posture toward that relationship? Does either one of them dismiss it as nice theory, but not realistic? Does Jerry insist upon a strictly transactional agenda between Melinda and himself rather than a willingness to focus on their relationship's vitality and future?

These four counter-indicators do not comprise a final list, certainly not if our agenda were primarily psychoanalytic rather than evangelical. But they may surface somewhere during your Conflict Redemption experiences.

I have encountered one or more of these counter-indicators in less than 5 percent of the church situations where I have worked on-site. Hardly an epidemic! If they do surface, *please* remember they are signals, not diagnostic conclusions. These are signals for more help from or through the church, if possible, in a Christ-Caring spirit!

Grouch Groupies and Antagonists

I laughed aloud while reading a delightful newspaper account of a woman who just defeated fifteen other nominees for "Grouch of the Year" honors in her small Texas town. She claimed the election was rigged since no one admits voting for her. Her husband, who was out of town at the time, said if he had been there she would have gotten twice as many votes.

Each neighborhood has its Top Crab, and so do congregations. Most parishes have one or more members who always seem to be on the pastor's case. So where is the problem? Regardless of age, *grouches* will always be with us. They are not sick, just inconvenient, annoying and sometimes embarrassing to a congregation. Bethany provides shelter for seven Grouches and four certified Antagonists. Antagonists are more troublesome than Grouches, since Grouches just *react*, usually episode by episode. Antagonists *scheme.* On the surface, their strategies resemble a sort of terrorism as their objective seems to be short-circuiting the congregation's systems, the Office of called and ordained Ministry, and vital relationships within Bethany. Antagonists are your spoilers.

Antagonists neither define nor cause church conflict, however. To imagine they do is a fundamental misunderstanding of church conflict and what can be done about it. Clergy and laity alike are deluded into fantasies that "everything will be all right if only we can get rid of such troublemakers." (If you have come this far in the book, that fallacy should be apparent.) Sorely disruptive problems can arise in congregations which allow their fellowship and function to be skewed or distorted by *antagonists*.

This happened at Bethany, and it signifies three things:

1. Bethany is not purpose-bonded; it is glued around emotional or family ties. Antagonists play on emotions; it is their tool-of-the-trade.

2. Bethany is vulnerable to Antagonists' influence to the degree it gets bogged down in maintenance ministry. Their ship is either dead-in-the-water or barely underway in today's heavy seas. Up on deck, loaded loose cannon are rolling around, firing at any handy target. Destination: uncertain. Crew and officers: confused. Most know their tasks, but why bother? Bethany had better figure out its destination, why it has to get there, the nature of its cargo, and recognize it is a *ship* rather than a small armada of spiritual kayaks! Otherwise, it will be easy prey for these pirate-type members already on board.

3. Bethany's awareness of its corporate personality and its bodily existence is shredded into the confetti of religious virtuosi or co-opted scabs from the surrounding culture. Too many churches think they have "factions" when, instead, they house *fragments*. Each fragment has its own agenda and expectations, each is a shrub lacking any sense of the forest. Spiritual Sandbox ecologies are where Antagonists flourish.

What To Do About Antagonists

If you unify and vivify the One New Person in your midst, Antagonists become little more than stinkweeds rather than the deadly virus you imagined they were.

Nothing dilutes Antagonists' influence and gambits better than two developments:

1. Move forward to get the congregation's *purposeful* act together, bonding and functioning around a pervasive system of *So Thats,* and

2. Respond to Antagonists for what they actually are: opportunities for resilient Christ-Caring ministries.

"What is *really* the matter, George?" asked privately in a Christ-Care spirit is at once a more effective and appropriate way of approaching Antagonists than is playing futile fight-fire-with-fire games.

Recognize that while Grouch Groupies can be annoying, Antagonists can become disruptive. How far these alien organisms can progress in infecting the Body depends so much upon how weakened that Body already is from prolonged purpose-starvation.

Afterword

Controls and power do have their validity, even within the church. As long as your Purpose System keeps them in their place, that is. Otherwise, they become an ego-serving exercise.

Power plays and control games never have the organization's best interests at heart, whether in church, business, or elsewhere. Unless they are overridden, these impulses drive either company or church toward bankruptcy—mission and spiritual bankruptcy above all. Unfortunately, ego-serving power players are not easily converted to team players. But their influence can be diluted, with an agenda which focuses your strategy.

What if mental illness components get involved with control games or other obstacles to church vitality? This rarely happens, but when it does, it is likely to follow a scenario on the periphery of a church's conflict situations. Where indicators point to the possibility of these components' presence, it means three things for you: put Conflict Redemption on hold relative to that person(s), do not play amateur psychiatrist, and synchronize specific aspects of Conflict Redemption with whatever the psychiatrist or psychotherapist advises.

ABOUT THE PARSONAGE "TRACK"

The format and schedule I have used for on-site Consultations includes a Saturday night dinner out with the pastor and spouse; often Sunday evening is added. These times have been one of the most satisfying features of my experience with Peace in the Parish! It is not easy for a parsonage to anticipate the arrival of this "expert;" it is somewhat like having another cook come into your kitchen. But when you come as an Audicator, as more help from the larger church, rather than as some conflict "mediator" between parsonage and parish, you can become an advisor and friend to that parsonage.

This is a "track" clearly distinct from one's advisory role with the congregation, I should add. (The distinction is quite appropriate in most mainline denominations since supervision of clergy is at least shared with— if not reserved to—the regional office/denomination which cooperated in my coming to that parish.) It helps that the region's leadership agrees that I share with them only my recommendations on next steps for that parsonage, usually with that couple's agreement.

In only one instance in nearly a hundred did I hit a brick wall; it was with the pastor rather than his wife. All of the others craved delight for their Calling, not to win or get even. I found no lusting after "success" but a yearning to get on with doing the ministry God had called them into long ago. As a husband and father, what lifts my own spirit has been to witness others who are as profoundly bonded to God's creation of their relationship as I have known with Loey!

12

Impacts of Immorality

◻

I t may have happened years ago, but it seems like only yesterday. Jake, a former pastor, was convicted of child-molesting. Mark, an admired music director, had an affair with a married woman choir member. Marvin took a shine to a much younger woman and divorced his wife who committed suicide less than a year later. Phyllis, an associate pastor's wife, left him for Julie, that congregation's Director of Evangelism. Bernadette, long-time treasurer from a stalwart family, is caught embezzling thousands of dollars from a congregation. Dr. Brown, the Head Elder, abandoned his wife and family and moved to San Francisco to live with his homosexual lover. These are a few samples of traumatic immorality in congregations where I have consulted. Does it sound more like Peyton Place than like the church?

Adjudication process for such offenses varies by denomination with official procedures bearing chiefly on transgression by clergy or other professional workers. Although I do not get involved in these procedures, I have been involved with the impacts of these events and the way things were handled. In several congregations, more devastation remained from how the local congregation or regional jurisdiction *dealt* with the matter than from the matter itself.

The media seems to gloat over such traumas. Their audience may feel less guilty about their own immorality when the church's seamy side is exposed. So what else is new beyond the technology that makes the exposure so quick and pervasive? No matter how hard we try to keep Satan from the church's front door, he keeps jimmying open side windows, prowling for the choicest catches.

With *Peace in the Parish*, our primary focus has been on how these traumatic episodes of immorality affect the congregation and its successive ministries. Here are some areas where intentional ministry is needed, with suggestions on coping redemptively with those episodes' aftermaths.

The Parish Dimension

When a professional Christian worker or lay leader's immorality is sexual, the impact on some members can be terrifying.

Christians are relentlessly pursued by Satan. Often this pursuit is accompanied by insidious rationalizations and minimalizations, rather than by outrageous frontal temptation. "It is not going to be that serious. I can call it off anytime. I can keep it separated from my marriage." People tend to flirt with the possibility, perhaps fantasize a trial run. Then they recoil, back off, come to their senses.

Then, the pastor or other church leader actually *does* what was still only a temptation for that Christian. Oh yes, indeed, we are appalled at the pastor. At the same time, a Christian is terrified of his or her own possibilities: "There, but for the grace of God, go I!" Many Christians sublimate the presence of their own base desires while corporately waging war against outside immorality. Then, *whoosh,* those hidden desires erupt in our midst, writ so large, so exposed.

Our marriages and family lives have their peaks and valleys, stresses and distresses. Friends divorce; a relative's child goes to prison; a nephew becomes a drug addict. Could this happen to *my* marriage or child?

At church, we crave assurance of our key relationships' well-being, almost as much as we crave assurance of salvation. A pastor or a fellow saint somehow embodies what is possible for a Christian marriage and family, in/with/under life's ordinary stresses and strains. We welcome and are encouraged by these visible assurance models. With such expectations of the church, clergy or lay leaders' immorality is an especially hard blow to any congregation.

CORPORATE EMBARRASSMENT AND DEMORALIZATION

These episodes of immorality resemble what we feel when somebody desecrates the flag: a mix of hurt, frustration and anger. Pastor Flirt has trifled with and violated the congregation's symbolic truth! Because ministry is a *public* office, a very public office, it carries a great deal of our unofficial freight. Contained in the freight cars are reputation, corporate culture, our children's attitudes and religious future, and narrowly defined Ordained-and-Called responsibilities.

Immorality among church professionals ravages the corporate equilibrium of congregations more quickly than anything else imaginable as it undermines the visible reliability of our belief-system.

Pastor Flirt

Holy Cross's long-time associate, Pastor Flirt, had been confronted by his seduction of and simultaneous affairs with three teenaged girls in the youth group. Later, it was discovered this had happened before in another jurisdiction.

The scandal broke one month into Pastor Stable's tenure as senior pastor. Pastor Flirt was immediately removed by the Bishop. Members pleaded with Pastor Stable to tell them how Christian doctrine works for them in all this. Interpret for us. Equip us. We need to know it is for real, and that it can heal.

When Pastor Stable was incapable of doing so, he was out of Holy Cross a year after arriving. He was unable to respond effectively to a real faith-crisis brought on by Pastor Flirt's immorality. With his *magisterium* or teaching authority gutted, the rest of his pastoral role also lost its credibility. He *had* to leave.

A few members take smirking comfort from clergy immorality. Their motto: "A pastor is only human." Their hidden agenda is: Therefore, I do not have to feel so guilty about what *I* am doing. Some codependent members may fix their eyes only on Pastor Flirt's holy achievements to the point that his immorality is barely noticed by their horse-blindered peripheral vision.

Several built-in problems should inform a congregation's agendas for handling the impacts of clergy or leader immorality. Adjudication decisions and measures are stipulated by your regional church jurisdiction, of course. Aside from those very few clergy with promiscuity problems, is there something about the parish ministry which can "set up" the naive and well-meaning pastor for sexual misconduct or worse?

Clergy Sexuality in Church Systems

Being a pastor is sexier than most Christians realize. Implicit to the ordained and called ministry's public character, this "sexiness" is distinct from whatever sex-appeal a pastor personally conveys. It may drag even the most unlikely and unattractive clergy into serious trouble. Ignore it at your peril, as far too many pastors and their spouses do. Tragedies seem to involve pastors who are hardly sex symbols, rather than those rare predatory wolves on clergy rosters.

As if personal lust-and-libido temptations were not enough to deal with, there are corporate impulses which focus sexual pressures on a pastor and/or parsonage. These pressures flow from within a congregation's core character as a church system, no less than from a church system's psycho-emotional fringes. Such sexual pressures flow along several distinct channels, sometimes intermingling, often imitating centuries-old patterns for ideological leaders.

How these church-system patterns and pressures differ between male and female professional church workers is, frankly, unknown. I am unaware of any significant data available on women's experience with such patterns. While this section describes typical sexual aspects of *male* leadership in church systems, you may discern some similarities and some mandates for further investigation into women's roles and dilemmas.

Our comments in Chapters 12 and 13 are organized in three segments:

- **Ideological leadership in church systems**

- **Seduction Scenario** (Chapter 13)

- **Responses**

Ideological Leadership in Church Systems

For reconciling the contradictions of Christian existence, we cling to the utter mystery of God's grace. For keying our behaviors around grace, we crave models. How can we do better than just live with these contradictions? We are encouraged by living embodiments of God's gracious presence in our messed-up life. One of these living embodiments may be our pastor, unless personal traits displace this reconciling embodiment we expect from the Office of ordained and called ministry.

Major systemic concerns have as much bearing as theological principles do on justifying the classic distinction between *Office* and *Person* in ordained ministry. Blurring or eliminating that distinction in favor of the *Person* can set up a pastor for erotic pressures which too few can withstand. For example, the Bakker and Swaggart episodes were tragically typical of what can happen when ideological leadership loses the *Office* under a snowballing dependence on a *Person's* gifts, skills, charisma and felt needs. Episodes of tension between Office and Person can chafe at the pastor and parsonage. However, that same tension discourages rationalizations over meeting some member's personal erotic needs. Doctrinally, there is a symphonic tension between *Person* and the *Office,* but adulterous or sex-perverted clergy neither play nor hear that symphony.

Bonding with the *Office,* which embodies the church's purposeful belief system, channels creativity away from eroticism which draws from the same well. Nonetheless, here are a couple of archetypes from ideological leadership that may illuminate why pastors can find themselves in some unexpected sexual predicaments.

LEADER AS HERO

Regarding the Pastor as Hero can produce some powerful erotic components. How does "Pastor" become "Hero"? The Hero label can emerge from a perception that things are going awfully well for the congregation since this pastor came here. He may become a Hero when a member's extended family has experienced strongly-appreciated personal blessing from his ministry. Hero also could be in the mix of a codependent relationship, or derived from charisma and public *persona*.

What happens next is a strange thing. Members bond with Pastor Hero in a curiously contradictory way which is at once idealizing yet demeaning when they: (1) regard this pastor's ministry as heroically lifting their church experience beyond previous expectations and (2) assign to this pastor the embodiment of what the church believes. Specifically, the Hero ideological leader is at once de-sexualized and yet hyper-sexualized.

1. De-sexualized

After years of congregational distress and trauma, my first parish was taking in new members almost every Sunday. When our first child was born, several active older ladies made it clear that they emotionally disassociated their new young "hero" pastor from our daughter's origination, as if she had been created by immaculate conception. They were *de-sexualizing* their ideological leader. Not rationally, of course.

De-sexualization originates from a variety of innermost tensions or aspirations. It moves on what psychologists call projection tracks. It also connects with people's confusion over good and evil in their own sexuality. When a member is de-sexualizing her male Pastor-Hero, the constraints and common sense governing her relationships with other men are suspended, including disassociation from her casual sexual overtones in your presence.

2. Hyper-sexualization

Hyper-sexualization can become a kind of self-fulfilling prophecy, as it was for James Jones (Jonestown) and for too many charismatic politicians. Without considering power-as-aphrodisiac complexities, hyper-sexualization describes the way members impute to their Hero a much higher degree of sexual attraction and capability than is humanly possible. Most powerfully triggered by fantasy related to the pastor's corporate *ritual* functions, the Hero's supporters can move back and forth between de-sexualizing him and hyper-sexualization.

During an insightful televised interview, an evangelist described how after exceptionally effective rallies he knew several attractive women would be waiting for him regardless which exit he took. These women were complete strangers. The man was remarkably candid in entering a rarely-treated topic until the show's host blurted out "Groupies!"

No, not Groupies; it is something more powerful and potentially destructive. For example, the erotic bonding process which happened between Adolf Hitler and his mass rally audiences has been noted by scholars. (When a speech went really well, Hitler is said to have remarked that it had suspended his "need of or interest in a woman.") It was the *event* rather than the speech's content which triggered the bonding.

This hyper-sexualizing bond with Pastor Hero happens when his ritual actions of speaking or preaching

galvanize *individuals* in the audience to create an intimacy with him amidst a corporate experience of a birth
of something bigger than all of us. This new-born's life
span may not last beyond the event's conclusion. But
the flicker of intimacy gets re-lighted each time an
individual member distorts even one-on-one brief encounters into ritual encounters. Right after such an
event, be wary of a gushy "Pastor, I *must* speak with
you!"

Clergy sometimes set themselves up for suspicion of
sexual misconduct. Pastors who do not *do* doctrine in
how they treat people devastate pastoral authority. In
a church system, a pastor must be a visible exemplar in
how one treats members of the opposite sex, especially
one's own spouse. Pastors demonstrate *how* what our
church believes works in this major dimension of
members' own lives: *sexuality,* not just in marriage and
family, but within the Body of Christ. I Timothy 3 and
Acts 7 come to mind as typical passages spelling out this
same point.

There are pastors who carry on infantile rebellions
against their congregation's behavioral expectations of
the pastor. This rebellion manifests itself in blatantly
foul language, drinking or other "liberated" activity.
What is actually going on is nothing but a cheap-shot
abdication of a biblical calling to the *Office* of Ministry.

We cannot carry over stereotypes from previous
generations. What does it mean to treat a lady like a
Lady in your congregation? Refrain from treating her as
one of the guys. Adversaries and allies both take note of
their pastor's day-to-day dealings with the opposite
sex. They may know the history of that particular member's troubled home life far better than Pastor does.
While Pastor is only being *caring,* members are being
historical. In your naivete', you complain they are being
hysterical.

Pastor Chuck and Sandra

During an On-Site Consultation, Pastor Chuck complained to me about how member alligators were impugning his relationship with Sandra, the Christian Education Director.

Sandra was visibly dedicated to her work at church. She was twice-divorced and had been indicted, but not convicted, on charges of carnal knowledge with a teenager. She was a long-time member; sixty years ago her grandparents became charter members.

Chuck had been pastor there for only three years. His wife had been told by a naively inexperienced seminary professor to refer to her husband only as "The Pastor" in conversation with members. Chuck's alligators saw how cold and cavalier he was to his wife. They observed the contrast of how caring and solicitous he was with Sandra. They also knew about the two hours Chuck spent with her in her office behind locked doors on a daily basis. Pastor Chuck fumed to me about how his *alligators* were undermining his ministry! Bright, gifted for ministry, but a real jerk nonetheless.

Pastor, lay people are not *stupid!* If you imagine she is keeping it confidential, let me assure you she is *not*. Unlike liaisons involving other professions, with an ideological leader she will try her insidious best to *destroy* you, your reputation, your US relationships and your ministry. This destruction will be by hints or by leaking inside information, especially if it can get back to your spouse.

Remember the life-sentenced pastor in CBS' "Murder Ordained?" He developed a caring relationship with a woman who reportedly had nearly *forty* other affairs in that Kansas community. She made sure that affairs in that Kansas community. She made sure that same community found out about her liaison with this pastor, however. (His wife and the other woman's husband were killed during this scandal).

Ideological leaders' hyper-sexualization by adversaries can be fueled by a congregation's and a parsonage's *collapsed* Purpose System, when claimed higher principles have been divorced from fickle preferences.

- *Caring* gets divorced from our highest aspirations, no longer done *to* and *because* of Christ, no longer *accountable* to Him, but done for fuzzies at the lowest purpose levels. Such caring folks are clutching their Ecclesiastical Binkies.

- When low-purpose adversaries observe a pastor's caring, they will put the worst construction on his actions, even when his efforts are led by higher purpose. When the operative corporate purpose system is trapped on the lower two dimensions, trouble comes as adversaries have easy access to a larger audience for their scurrilous complaints.

- So it is not a simple matter of whether or not the pastor's *caring* is sinful, but why is the congregation so vulnerable to worst-possible-case interpretation?

The more obsessed you are with your own needs, the less realistic you become about the church's limits and your *own* behavioral limits in relating to members of the opposite sex. This decaying realism often can be seen in how you use autobiographical components in preaching and teaching. Angry preachers are often very Law-driven. The Gospel they do utter is unrelated to the Law. Why? Because that Gospel is disconnected from the anger crippling their own lives.

Pastors often overlook how perceptive some members are in picking up on clues that sermons scatter about when you think you are only using the Law. These may be biographical clues, vulnerability clues, pathways for seduction. I have been amazed at how many ministerial adulteries got set up when the person in the pew picked up on such clues from the pastor's sermons or teaching.

Great preachers throughout history have made marvelous use of autobiographical material in their sermons. It is helpful for members' appropriating the message to their own lives, and it helps them discern how well their pastor has claimed the message in parsonage and personal experience. While homileticians—teachers of preaching—have a point in urging pastors to be careful with autobiography material in sermons, I might suggest a simple principle which can help you use it appropriately. If it illustrates only Law, watch out!

Be explicit in how autobiographical material directly keys to your own *Gospel* outcomes. In my experience, pastors who employ such material in Law-bound ways are too often soliciting or reinforcing codependency. Or they may be sending out seduction signals, even as they imagine they are being "prophetic." A *very* close second place to autobiographical mishaps is how preachers proclaim social concerns with a Law-driven dogmatism which at least equals the pietistic dogmatisms of others.

In counseling, recall the warnings you have read and heard about in courses. Especially noteworthy are three principles:

- A pastor always must set the limits in counseling situations, including need to diminish possibilities of fantasy impulses about you by the counselee.
- Never indulge your own self-disclosure impulses with counselees, regardless of how hurting or badly

you feel. The exception is to relate only clearly Gospel-illustrative examples.

- Tactile counseling is too volatile. Quit all that touchey-feeley stuff, preacher! Hug your own spouse, not somebody else's.

PASTOR AS PREDATOR

When a male pastor becomes sexually involved with an adult member, regardless of how much consent or initiative she brings to the affair, the church must regard it as nothing less than sexual abuse. By the pastor! Whether or not the affair includes intercourse, and along with its sinful character and violation of the Office, the matter must be dealt with as an abuse case. The analogy is quite close to parent/adult-and-child abuse scenarios, because both situations include corrupt uses of power. Specifically, that pastor is manipulating psycho-emotional corollaries of religious regard for the pastor. From his power position, he is turning her respect for or dependence on her pastor into Herr Pastor's assault on her vulnerabilities.

Responses for the Injured Parish

1. Face the hurts and angers

First of all, face those angers which were generated in your congregation by the immorality episode. Face not only the corporate impacts but also the direct and rippling wave-like effects on members. Regard this time as an occasion for concerted effort to experience the full range of what we believe at work! (Refer to Chapter 2 on Doctrine for a sense of how you can approach this agenda.) Then adapt a *Congregation Bond of Peace Service* (see Chapter 15) to focus this process when all of you are ready to bring it to closure. If you do not bring those hurts and angers to closure, they will remain an obstacle to vitality in the future as the past runs amok.

2. Ministry for Victims

Thus far, denominational/regional jurisdictions have usually moved decisively and firmly in cases of clergy sexual abuse of minor children. There is no excuse for not being just as decisive about clergy sexual misconduct with adult members, whether heterosexually or homosexually.

- The affair is a form of murder whose victims include more than that member. Betrayed and under attack are the One New Person relationships of the pastor and Other Person, the members of the Body of Christ "US" in that congregation, institution, as well as the church at large.

- Forgiveness is offered no less to murderers than to the rest of us. For the church, however, forgiveness must not be manipulated into a qualification for re-entering parish ministry. I have heard more than a few sexually-abusing clergy (and spouses) whine that "our church does not *believe* in forgiveness." We certainly do! We also believe in justice for victims, in caring for—and safeguarding—the Body, building up the Office of Ministry's integrity. Ministry is a public Office, but not a public bus where anybody who pays the fare or dues can get on board and take any available seat.

    In other words, personal forgiveness becomes counterfeit when it becomes a transaction for staying on or restoration to the clergy roster.

• Thank God if a clergy sex-abuse episode is truly a first-and-only incident. Most often, however, it is not the first, nor is it the last. Years ago, judicatories could get away with moving offenders to another parish Call. ("All I want is another chance, Bishop.") In today's climate, not only with a public awareness but reflex-litigation, how much jeopardy should we impose upon the church?

Give timely support for spouses, children and friends of that troubled marriage, ministry and family. Public and personal support in a no-fault spirit must be given to all One New Persons surviving the tragedy. There should be no tolerance for comments such as: "If only she had been a better wife, Pastor would not have been tempted." (People who say this may be looking for their *own* exploits' excuse!) The stronger the codependency or the higher the pedestal on which a member has placed a pastor, the more tempted one is to say such things. Anticipate and carefully counsel these members' deflections of responsibility.

3. Minister to fears

While a detailed picture may not yet be visible, minister to fears with a broad brush. Strong support for marriage is a high priority in most of these situations. Emphasize Bible study about One New Person relationships. Bring in other teaching and informational resources. Consider possibilities for couple or family retreats, including a weekend program at the church if travel to another center is not feasible.

4. Office of Ministry

Distinct from the person in it, the *Office* of Ministry will suffer irreparable damage if the episode is not directly addressed. Since this is a public office, specific steps for repentance and redress of damages must include that *public* dimension, along with whatever the private docket involves. What has to happen for the health of the Body of Christ here is no less important than individuals' needs.

What about a "rehabilitated" offender? How reliable are professional reassurances of rehabilitation? Often I am asked by regional church leaders whether immoral clergy can "fool" a professional counselor. The answer is an emphatic "Yes!" These days, it is virtually automatic for church authorities to impose 20th-century Protestant penance on erring clergy: x-amount of counseling. But at least four factors often torpedo this strategy:

a) intellectual/IQ mismatch, with the pastor being much brighter than the counselor;
b) highly developed con artist traits of seducer-clergy;
c) past courses on counseling have shown seducer-clergy the right buttons to push if they get caught;
d) when the regional church authority surrenders its own Christian common sense in agreeing to abide by some counselor's out-of-context judgement.

5. Be Wise as Serpents

A strong reminder is in order about *how* public dimensions are to be dealt with. *Lawsuits mean never having to say you are sorry.* But too many congregations leave themselves wide open to the possibility of lawsuits.

a) Not only must the evangelical *spirit* of Matthew 18:15-20 be visibly honored in each official and

public action by the congregation, but clear iden-
tification of these actions with your Christ-Care
and overriding purposes is essential.

b) Declarations and procedures must take care to
avoid stepping over boundaries into either malicious injury to reputation or unlawful deprivation of livelihood, two of the favored grounds for
litigation against congregations. Violation of
due process as established by customs within the
church's tradition, by American jurisprudence
and of common Christian decency are frequently
court-cited mistakes in how churches handle
corporate impacts of immorality.

c) Regardless of your denomination's polity, do
not try to handle these litigation-prone aspects of
the matter solely on your own as a congregation.
Where professional help or treatment is necessary before that pastor or worker can be restored
to good standing in your denomination's roster,
assistance and cooperation by your regional jurisdiction is crucial. Otherwise, the congregation
acting on its own may leave itself open to that
deprivation of livelihood charge.

Above all, recognize that *how* a congregation deals
with the impacts of clergy or leader immorality and the
immoral action itself is at once a measure and model of
how our belief *works*.

The theory of the relationship between Law and
Gospel, God's judgment and love, repentance and new
life may elude the grasp of too many members. Our
basic belief will be understood, not by mere words, but
in seeing *how* we put our doctrine to work in such
difficult circumstances.

I am reminded of an ancient saying which some
ascribe to a contemporary of Paul, Rabbi Akiba: "Evil

originates among us whenever the quality of judgment exceeds the quality of mercy." And, vice versa. At each deliberate step taken, each action tabled or referred, ask each other: "Does this decision embody the whole of what we believe?"

Where does all this leave us—congregation, regional jurisdictions, denomination? I believe it leaves us to rely on two principles:

    a) evangelical common sense, and

    b) focused Christian compassion.

Afterword

The everyday ecology of Church and Ministry can provide sexually predatory pastors with opportunity, victims and erotic power they might not come by as readily in other positions. But it also can set up otherwise faithful and conscientious clergy for sexual liaisons they probably never intended. Naivete' about sex is far less of a problem than is naivete about ministry's strange capability to put male pastors in a "power position" with some vulnerable women parishioners. If an affair ensues, with or without intercourse, the pastor must take full responsibility for what amounts to a case of sexual abuse.

What happens next? First, church authorities have to take times and decisive action about any such episode of immorality by clergy or other professional church workers. No less important, however, is dealing with the episode's impacts on others, which requires deliberate action and even more evangelical compassion—especially toward victims, their relationships, and toward the Body of Christ. That compassion dissipates if it is neither timely nor substantive.

13

Parsonage Concerns

I t has been only during the last generation that parish
ministry ceased being an hereditary occupation. For
centuries, most Protestant clergy entered ordained ministry with their eyes open, already experienced with the
limits and delights of living in somebody else's house
(parsonage), as well as that household's give-and-take
with the place next door (parish). A pastor might be on
a housing allowance these days and be worrying about
mortgage payments. Regardless of ownership, there is
more mystery about parsonage households than about
members', and not just because clergy families are used
to seeing the Ideological Leader going around in under-
wear.

In this chapter's first section, we turn to an experience
most clergy households would assume could happen
only to some other parsonage: a pastor's affair with a
member of their parish. Yes, it is rare enough; no, not
even homely preachers are immune. We are not referring to sex abuser Predator Pastors mentioned previ-
ously, but rather to clergy who were not "on the prowl"
when the relationship started to snowball.

Seduction Scenario

It does happen. A fine, hard working and highly motivated pastor ends up in a messy extra-marital affair, which was the farthest thing from that pastor's mind when the relationship started. While details and drives vary among seduction situations, the following scenario is all too common.

- **Vulnerability**
- **Insinuation**
- **Alienation**
- **Execution**

1. Vulnerability

In adult life, probably the most vulnerable times for either pursuing or being open to extra-marital "intimacy" are junctures which pose significant increase in a person's bonding to spouse, family responsibility or vocation. This could be the birth of a child, a relationship-traumatizing death, or a major vocational change (not only a perceived big boost but a severe disappointment or disillusionment, as well).

Whether it is arrival of your first or fifth child, planning has to include a couple's deliberate, mutual understanding of how parenting will affect their Marriage US. What will both of you do to keep your Family-Marriage-Vocation One New Persons *in symphony* rather than in that disastrous hierarchy of priorities? How will both of you collaborate and support each other to prevent either/or predicaments among your God-given US relationships?

Gene

Gene was far less gifted than he had been brought up to believe. To steward those gifts, his wife had worked more than full-time throughout their seminary years so Gene could concentrate on preparing for what his extended family was sure would become a nationally famous ministry.

Gene was embarrassed by how entry-level his first parish really was, but he faithfully plodded along. There did not seem to be much opportunity for him to produce impressive statistics. By no fault of his, a major corporation located a new plant in his rural area, bringing in 2,000 new jobs and households. The church doubled its membership in just three years. Gene stayed on a bit longer than he had planned in order to harvest a statistical bumper crop.

Halfway across the country, another congregation under the influence of statistical hallucinogens called Gene. He saw this as a big promotion, a climb several rungs up the reputation ladder. Within a year after his arrival, Gene shed his wife and twin toddlers for another woman from an old-line family in the new community, someone who fit better into Gene's image of the successful pastor.

Parsonage Purpose System collapse usually is a key driving force in conflicts between career and home.

One clue: Are either of you forcing decisions into either-or battles or into priority pyramids? Is it a matter of ministry is first, marriage second, and children get the leftovers? Too many pastors and parsonages think they are *so* dedicated because they let Parish tyrannize Parsonage, as though "God will get you" if you *ever* allow your God-created Marriage US to interfere with Kingdom Work. Remember what we considered earlier about *making symphony*, so that your decisions *and* compensations play in harmony.

Or, there is the parsonage in which the pastor spends as much time babysitting his children as he spends in his ministry. "You have finished school; now it is my turn" is a common excuse, despite the fact neither of you would get away with this if you were working for somebody other than the church.

Whatever angers and tensions ensue from a parsonage's collapsing Purpose System are secondary to a larger common threat among sexually-transgressing clergy: De-valuation of your One New Person relationships and *inflation* of personal preference purposes (i.e. "my personal needs"). A Christian who lets an US get downgraded, who mutes or silences its melody in the larger symphony, loses perspective and becomes a sitting duck for the Deceiver.

The greatest vulnerability factor may be when a pastor or parsonage's identity is primarily with "Pastor" rather than *in Christ.* The more obsessed you become with the activities of ministry, the less importance your US relationships will have for you, including your US in Christ. Do you pray more and harder for your ministry than for your marriage? That is what happens when you exist to *perform* more than to *conform* to God's compassionate love in Christ Jesus.

Pastor, do you feel you are doing better at church than at home? *Much* better? If so, it is time to rearrange your attention and money resources, including continuing education, to get matters back in harmony. It is so seductive to let yourself wallow in church rather than care for that US at home, especially when you get so many more strokes from church members than from family. Are you letting your self-esteem get co-opted by the "pastor" business? The deeper you sink into this quagmire, the more vulnerable you are to alienation from your Marriage and Family US's.

2. Insinuation

I have yet to meet a pastor whose involvement with the Other Person got *started* on an affair track. Invariably, it begins on a pastorally proper route, a route defined by your situation, not hers.

Counseling is the seduction track most often thought to be the culprit. Seminary professors, colleagues, reading materials and pastoral conferences have given pastors so much advice on safeguards that, if you do get involved with a counselee, the assumption is it happened by deliberate intent. Nonetheless, I am no longer sure that counseling is the most common occasion for these affairs.

The tactical factor seems to be activity which brings Other Person (OP) into frequent and increasingly private company with the pastor. The key strategic element is appeal to the pastor's caring role or propensity for caring, especially if a pastor is naive or not Christ-centered enough to know when it is time to remove himself from the situation.

—*Volunteer work:* OP takes on only those aspects of church work which are known to be pet concerns of the pastor. This work entails a high enough level of effort to earn pastoral responses like "You are such a help."

Usually, Other Persons are *chameleons,* intended or not. They take on or blend into a church's language and mannerisms with remarkable facility. This is all the more remarkable when you consider how this behavior contrasts sharply with OP's prior ecology.

—*Part-time staff:* We hear stories about bosses becoming involved with their secretaries, but this appears to be less likely for adulterous pastors. Pastors are more prone to become involved with someone through a *collegial* relationship which, in most churches, is quite possible on part-time bases. Seduction-vulnerable pastors tend to become the *competitor,* rather than colleague, in relationships with other *full*-time professional workers. Competition is not exactly the best atmosphere for seduction, is it?

3. Alienation

Alienation precedes most adulteries. This alienation often starts with the US relationship that was most formative for your Purpose System. By the way, your Marriage US is probably *not* going to be the first item on the Alienation Agenda, if only because your Purpose System formation likely preceded the wedding. Most often, the primary target will be your family of origin, unless it was abusive or destructive.

I notice the most far-reaching work of alienation occurs during each pull-back period. You have "ended it." "We are going to be Just Friends." So you have pulled back from letting the OP relationship go any farther. But it does go farther! When you are involved with a Chameleon, he or she knows that pull-back is just a temporary color change. Besides, when you are in a Just Friends mindset, your defenses are less alert to alienation ploys.

You notice shortcomings in your One New Persons, flaws which never really bothered you until Other Person came along. Why *did* God join you together with people who are not "meeting my needs"? The road to an US murder is paved with "unmet needs"!

Avoidance surfaces. Other friends, Righteous Ones who care about you, approach and try to get through to you. "I just cannot talk about it now." Of course not, because "It" is the homicide that is happening, and your life has come apart at the core. Too many pieces are yet to be sorted out to be able to discuss what has happened. Self-deceiving excuses and rationalizations are starting to surface, trying to twist demonic murder of One New Persons into a case of justifiable homicide.

A Christian US *can* die more often by its starvation and abusive neglect than by frontal assault conspiracy. God's Word does demand that such a death must not be by murder! This murderous assault on other US relationships (e.g. your Parenting/Family US) is common among too many divorced people who prefer scapegoating to confessing their own part as at least accomplice (if not co-conspirator) to a Marriage US murder.

4. Execution

Rather than merely reflecting the deed's first offspring of pain, confusion and guilt, persistent avoidance signals that the alienation has succeeded. You avoid places and environments where the dead US and your other One New Persons used to live. As this happens, you become more isolated from them and more dependent on Other Person, so that your alienation from them snowballs and accelerates. While you may fantasize that you can re-create those One New Persons in adjustment to your liaison with Other Person, need we remind you that only *God* creates an US? You may do patchwork realignments. You may even experience a tidbit of "staying on good terms." But do not be deceived into thinking these are any more than low-level relationships.

Genital sex may still be absent from the relationship, especially if you have made its absence a clean White

Robe to cover up the carnage. Counselors who have worked with troubled clergy marriages will agree that in these described scenarios, alienation preceded sex, which often remained the Big No-No for quite some time after the assassinations were done. Do not nurture the deception that because there has been no sex, everything else with Other Person is harmless. Nobody should assume that genital sex is the only or most common weapon for murdering an US.

If this section registers, you probably realize by now that: (a) powerful sexual components are written into the script for murdering a pastor's marriage US, even without genital sex; and (b) you do not have to be an Agatha Christie to figure it out.

Is the answer to shun friendships and working relationships with the opposite sex? By no means! If so, Christian life would have to scurry off into segregated monasteries and convents. The basic principle for *Christian* relationships is quite simple: *In Christ.* From this your clear sense of ethics and morals, of your US's origination and objectives, and all other lesser considerations take their single reference point for sound judgment. Christians who discern the magnificent reality of their One New Person relationships have taken the next step in translating *in Christ.* This will be their delight and lead their conduct in otherwise ordinary contact with others.

SUGGESTIONS AND SAFEGUARDS

1. Trinity Model

Regard the Trinity as a model for Marriage and for rightly relating all your One New Persons. Is one US person *over* the others? That is not how the three Persons in the Trinity relate, is it? Your US relationships are distinct instruments and distinct melodies; here one soars for several bars, then it recedes while another soars. But this is done in symphony.

2. Purpose System

While quite healthy at the outset of ministry, some parsonage Purpose Systems collapse in the poisonous vacuum of destructive anger. There is no shortage of understandable worry in parsonages. This worry typically is generated by financial pressures worsened by heavy school debts. In this case, we are pointing beyond worry to the kind of *anger* which seduces the parsonage into a decisive obsession with "needs."

Figure out what your Purpose System is for your parsonage, starting with three important concerns—

a) Are your children learning the family's Purpose System by clear degrees of discipline (e.g. when a spanking is guaranteed), by the consistent futility of playing Mom and Dad against each other, by how you allocate limited time and money resources to nourish your Marriage US? How do you nourish the family's corporate spiritual life? How do you nurture the spiritual lives of individuals in the household?

b) Are both of you committed to keeping your One New Persons in symphony? Is there a clear policy on compensating your other US relationships when one has to be the dominant melody for a while? When a parish emergency forces you to delay a marriage or family event, do you make timely decisions on how and when to match the level of disappointment with an equivalent experience?

c) Does the household actually experience your Purpose System working in how you discuss and deal with parish conflict? What sorts of things frustrate or set you off the most, the least, and what principles *actually* govern how you sort out the matter? Do your reactions provide a lesson in prudent use of your Purpose System? Or, are your parish and parsonage relationships mired in either/or legalism?

My Day Off

The head elder's wife had a massive heart attack. Specialists said the next two hours were critical. The elder called his pastor, asking this recent seminary graduate to be with them in this crisis. Asked to be God's Man, this character instead recalled a professor's rule: "Protect your day off." He told the Elder, "Call somebody else. Today is my day off." True story!

3. Build Play into your Purpose System

Commit yourselves to generate and nourish the element of redemptive *surprise* in your life together, or you will become dull to the Gospel's surprises. You are never too poor to afford candles for a Dinner for Two. Romance injected into the midst of an unavoidably trying day of parenthood and vocation is welcome. Embody the Gospel when rules have to be enforced. Seek out marriage friends with whom you enjoy being silly, who will not or cannot advance your career one inch. Enjoy a movie which lacks one iota of theological significance. Getting the idea?

4. Physical health

What is your witness to Christ in how others see you caring for your body? You are too spiritual for that?

Well then, you are not playing with a full deck—biblically! Do this: Focus a full month of your personal Bible study on how God's Word regards caring for our physical bodies. Gross overweight and disdain for healthful exercise turn you into an ambulatory insult to Stewardship, at the least!

5. Deal with old hurts

Parsonages horde hurts like squirrels hoard nuts, going back to that first Call in Pigstye, New Hampshire. When similar hassles came up at tonight's Council meeting, it was as if somebody had flicked a switch to energize an array of short-circuits connecting to way back. Pastor and spouse, it is high time you claim for yourselves and for your parsonage that biblical blessing of Forgetting old hurts. Get another parsonage couple to go with you to the altar: Bind those hurts and angers, let go of them, hand them over to our Lord of Time, Alpha-and-Omega!

When Luther invented the parsonage, it was not with celibate cohabitation in mind. Ever since that Wittenberg parsonage, clergy households have lived their own version of what *Public* Ministry can too often mean. I have been inspired by the powerful love I have seen at work in most parsonages. Tragically isolated, alone, confused by what has been happening during times of church conflict, these pastors' homes have been revelations to me. They mirror what it means to be bonded to God-created US relationships, just as I have known with my beloved wife and our children throughout all kinds of hardship. Parsonages are glass-house laboratories of what is possible for Christian marriages and families in your congregation.

Parsonage Stress

While we were a parsonage family in three different parishes, we had the feeling that other clergy households were strangers to the kind of high-stress experience we had. The years in graduate school component added some stresses that perhaps other parsonage families did not endure. We socialized with groups of Chicago-area pastor couples, and they did not show much wear and tear. At conventions when asked, "How's it goin'?" some clergy replied as though they were hawking a breakfast cereal: "Guh-rayt!"

Then, one couple divorced. A year later, another couple divorced. Two pastors virtually ran from the parish into "specialized ministry," complaining of "too much stress and frustration." But everything was always "Just Great!" Thank God, most of our early parish colleagues continue in faithful church ministry.

Three years ago, through a broad-based sample of Lutheran parsonages (over 400 clergy households in four states participated), we investigated parsonage stress factors. We developed both an instrument ("Parsonage Concerns Inventory") and an analytic computer program to process information. Since the project was unfunded, we were unable to convene groups or do follow-up interviews. Our research not only sought to profile parsonage stressors but to rank their intensity.

By combining Parsonage Concerns Inventory results with my observations from extended interviews with pastors and spouses, research-based sketch of contemporary parsonage stress is clear enough to summarize at this point.

SURPRISES AND ASSURANCES

A number of parsonage household stereotypes of generations ago have eased, if not eroded, into exceptions. With so much media attention recently focused on so-called "competency" levels or on scandals among clergy rosters, there are signs that today's pastor has important strengths that our grandparents' preachers seemed to lack. For example, we have noticed:

1. *Marriage and ministry symphony*—The old saw of Ministry first and all else (marriage, family) on a descending priority scale did not prevail in our sample, regardless of age, from near-retirement to newer clergy households. Indeed, it was difficult to find any respondent using a "hierarchy of values" to relate parsonage and parish. Items—

   • 95 percent of the pastors said they would resign their current Call and seek another, if it meant saving their marriage.

   • 95 percent of the pastors said his wife (all clergy respondents were male) was his best and surest ally in the ministry. Ninety percent of the spouses also felt the parish's expectations of her were appropriate. Fewer (75 percent) felt well informed about conflicted situations in the congregation.

   • However, 17 percent of the pastors reported that their wives had become rigid and inflexible about the day off.

   • Nearly half the spouses felt "trapped" by their current situation.

2. Collegiality and trust among clergy (and parsonages) are breaking down. Items—

   • Over half agreed with this statement: "Our pastors

have become more *competitors* than colleagues with each other." Over half also agreed with: "There is much less trust with other pastors/spouses than we need."

- Twenty percent felt they were experiencing more difficulty than those who were at seminary with them.

- Over half felt more isolated now from reliable friends and support than ever before; nearly 60 percent said their best and most trusted friends lived far away.

- Single pastors (9 in our sample) felt this problem of isolation rather strongly. All cited "loneliness" as a key stress factor for them.

3. It was quite obvious that most parsonage couples took their "romantic life" seriously. Items—

- 90 percent of both husbands and wives said the other does "her (or his) part keeping romance alive in our marriage."

- But there were some interesting footnotes. Twenty-nine percent of these male pastors agreed with the statement: "There are times when I do feel the celibate/unmarried priesthood has its better points."

- 20 percent said that while their household is very important to them, "it has become less of a haven or refuge for me than I need."

- 20 percent of these pastors wished their wives "would take better care of her physical condition, grooming and appearance." Fifteen percent of the wives felt the same way about their husbands.

- Nearly 30 percent of their spouses felt the pastor was "naive" about women members.

STRESS FACTORS

"The rest of America is going through that, too." List the range of stress factors present in parsonages, and you are likely to get some version of that response. However, from our on-site experience and through the parsonage research project, the major variable which distinguishes the impact of parsonage stress from the general population's is that parsonages traditionally and currently rely much more on satisfaction wages. (You doubt it? Then you have not listened in on church Budget committees!) This reliance has been sorely compromised by the recent surge in church conflict, church litigation, and members' rising expectations of their church and its clergy. As clergy satisfaction wage scales decline, impacts of such stress factors multiply.

Indeed, I have noticed that one of the high fiscal costs of church conflict follows that old company principle: the worse the job, the higher the pay. The more church conflict chokes off staff satisfaction, the less likely they are to give their best (or, even stay around) unless dollars "compensation" soars to match levels of dissatisfaction. I heard one council member, herself no slouch at finance, explode at another member across the table who was known for his excessive frugality with church expenditures *and* who was jumping all over the pastor again: "You cost us too much! We are shelling out too much money to make up for all the misery you put our staff through!" And, when I investigated just a bit, she was *so* right.

There is a point to this. Denominational leaderships are sitting on a time bomb called: parsonage school debts. As a seminary professor taking my turn on the financial aid committee, I was appalled: the average indebtedness of students asking for aid was already over $14,000! Ten percent of the 400+ pastors in our sample graduated with "more than" $10,000 in school debts, not counting car loans.

Two related developments occurred in the late 1950's. Denominational bureaucracies—and their cost—multiplied like rabbits. To help pay for this indulgence, churches either started charging seminary tuition and fees for the first time in their history, or started piling more of seminaries' costs on to the students. "But other professional schools and universities were doing it." True. *But* their graduates were going to work for somebody else, not for the school's sponsor and constituency. Churches used to see their seminaries as an essential service to the church and its mission. The church is the seminary consumer, not the student. Yet, the finances no longer follow this fact. Meanwhile, seminary graduates are entering a compensation mindset which lags far behind this denominationally imposed deficit.

1. *Financial Stress Factor:* 40 percent of the sample parsonages ranked this in the "most severe" category, with a total of 79 percent saying it was a major stress in their lives. Parallel to this was another stress which I think is more closely related to financial worry than many may realize—

2. *Recognition deficiencies* and "being hassled by members." Seventy percent for the first item and 68 percent for the latter one were the sample's rating as "significant" stressors. 24 and 22 percent ranked them at the "highest" intensity stress level.

3. "But what a wonderful Pension program we have now for our professional Christian workers." Oh? Then, why did 24 percent of our sample rank "their financial future" at the highest stress intensity level, and 75 percent of them experience it at a "significant" stress level?

4. *Hurts and frustrations.* When a congregation "gets rid" of a pastor, the next congregation pays the bill. Then, the first church Calls another pastor...who just came from a "get rid of" situation! There is some justice to that, I suppose. But too much clergy "mobility" is fueled by congregations' down-right self-centeredness, their lacking a sense of responsibility toward their pastor's *future* parishes.

As we have noted earlier, parsonage hurts are more parish contextual than biographical. Our extensive sample bore this out. Fifty-one percent of our sample parsonages stated that their most strongly felt "past hurts" were parish-related.

Thus far, we have extracted several results from a preliminary research effort. (Given how much the larger church, no less than the local parish, has at stake in the integrity of its parsonages, the lack of serious attention to how parsonage households are doing is a rather large matter to let fall through the cracks!) Drawing from these findings and from my rather intensive personal interviews with many parsonage couples, what steps can be suggested? What can be done, now, about these matters?

Unfortunately, given mainline denominations' decline, and "independents'" general disregard for clergy well-being, too much of the "What's-to-be-done about parsonage vitality" falls on parsonages themselves. At least this is the reality until your denomination bids farewell to the diet of high-fad causes clogging its arterial system and is able to pay closer attention to its parsonages. I am more optimistic than many others are that this can happen. Why? Two related reasons lead that optimism. First, the usual time-lag is coming due, the lag between what is going on in the real world of management and what informs church management. That means denominations will have to catch up with the obsession with *service* which drives the more successful companies. Too much denominational thinking remains trapped in "program" and problem-staffing sloughs, with direct service getting leftovers. In the church, the harsh reality against this distortion is that constituent loyalty [and dollars!] flow toward where the most significant direct *service* originates. Surely, service to "client" congregations and parsonages rank high on that Service list. In the meantime, there remains that time-lag.

Well, what can be done? Besides marrying a magnificent *and* wealthy spouse or serving only those parishes which think you are the greatest thing since sliced bread?

1. If you need help from the larger church, your best bet probably is with your regional office. In the larger denominations, do not count too much on that. There are so many other pressures that undermine their response to parsonage concerns.

2. If your regional leadership is concerned about its parsonages (and most of those I know well among Lutherans are), two do-able needs can be addressed. First, strengthen clergy *and* parsonage collegiality by every trivial and major means possible! From golf

tourneys to text-study groups to how parsonages see the leadership devoting its time. For starters, that last point includes a higher percentage of time actually visiting on-site with parish clergy.

Second, regional judicatories must insist, at least, on due process according to Matthew 18—from various clergy no less than from laity. How can your pastors and spouses talk with each other if you permit an atmosphere of mistrust? If your office listens to tattle-tales which come your way via violation of those six verses, the "word" gets around quickly on what information actually guides your office.

3. Deal with your parsonage isolation and/or loneliness as a top priority. If your own denomination has been the scene of controversy, or if its pastors near you are in a competitor mode, I strongly urge parsonage folk to seek good friends in other denominations. Disloyal? No way! Since when is it "disloyal" to be a faithful steward of your God-created marriage and family One New Persons, and of your Vocation US? Remember that parsonages in *other* denominations have virtually nothing to gain professionally from tattle-tailing on you folks. Yet, chances are they do know what it is like, what you are going through.

- But, also keep your friendships light-hearted. I notice a direct correlation between "play" and collegiality amidst tragedy. Aristotle was right, as far as he went in his *Poetics:* tragedy and comedy both turn on the element of surprise. I would add: so does creativity, which does the surprising thing with what exists. Move well along the first two wave lengths and you are positioned for the third:

creativity. Good friends and colleagues who laugh together about their actual situation not only can better empathize with each other but become more open for God's surprises, for divine creativity! By definition, parsonages also exist to embody the Gospel's surprises: we get from God what we do not deserve. Surprise!

- If there are complaints to share, focus them on your parishes because you might be able to do something about that. To be sure, 17 percent of our sample felt a high degree (63 percent felt "some") frustration over a pastor's perceived "underutilization of gifts and skills for ministry" in a current setting. Does that constitute sure and certain proof that the Holy Spirit has forsaken your denominational superiors (and their Call "lists")? Probably not. It probably points up your frustration over isolation and to the whole system's bankruptcy for paying satisfaction wages.

4. Christ-Care begins with those you know. For parsonage couples, Christ-Care begins in the parsonage. Sure, that spouse of yours may no longer be the Ultimate Yum-Yum he or she was when you "got serious." Your thighs now look like Quonset huts. Where did all his hair go? Is that *really* a pulpit blister bulging above your belt? But God already created something wonderful, nonetheless, from you two. Bigger than both and alive beneath all the worry: a miracle, a superb, a special One New Person! Put all you believe to work on that US of yours. So that you can delight not only in a ministry that is making a difference, but in a marriage and household beloved of God. This is the greatest treasure you have!

Afterword

I am impressed by how many models for analysis pale before the mystery of the Body of Christ wherein we experience how God makes one-plus-one equal three. Alongside the constancy of that miracle there remains a nagging variable which makes efforts such as this book tragically necessary. The Body is wounded when its members regard their congregations as some sort of self-serve gas station where we refuel our private pick-up trucks for trips along the Highway of Life. In Scripture, do branches connect with the vine occasionally or temporarily? Of course not. Yet that is what we are faced with in the reality of congregational life. As long as it is so, we need reminders like this chapter to discern how the church is at once the Body of Christ while still a sinful Church System.

14

More Help from the Church

———— ▭ ————

Most parish consultations are actually done by regional offices of denominations. A congregation gets into trouble and calls for help. For example, among Lutherans that means the response happens under auspices of the District or local Synod office. Various denominations have ventured into the training of on-site teams for regional jurisdictions. These volunteer groups go into a local church to help it deal with conflict.

After working intensively with so many congregations myself, it may be helpful to list and explain some procedural Do's-and-Don't that I have learned. My hope is that this will encourage the spirit and effectiveness of such teams. While these observations are numbered, no order of priority is intended. Rather, it is for ease in reference and discussion.

On-Site Consultation

PREPARATION

Preparation in the congregation is extremely important. The on-site consultation group may know what it can and cannot do and what it is looking for. But the group's best intentions will blow up in its face if intensive preparation has not happened before they arrive. What kind of preparation?

1. A comprehensive set of resources has to be made available to the congregation at least six weeks prior to the event. It can be sent earlier, if the set will help informed voting on whether to have you come.

2. We use a four-part set of helps.
   a) Communications material includes several versions of every-member letters; five separate paragraphs for insertion into the Sunday bulletins, each week prior to the event.
   b) We include three copies of a 45-minute introductory videotape (two tapes are loaned). The tape is shown to groups, to open meetings, and can be borrowed for home viewing. In most congregations using this process, many key members will take it upon themselves to view the tape three to six times.
   c) A congregational *Coordinator's Folio* spells out in detail what to do, when and how. It includes a section of answers to questions most frequently asked by Coordinators.
   d) A complete sample set of recommended Bible studies (an essential follow-up emphasis), explanatory folders, hand-outs, and copies of a four-page / single-sheet printed Consultation sequence is sent.

VOTE AND COORDINATION

Simply having the Church Council approve a consultation puts the occasion on shaky ground. If at all possible, the congregation should vote. Several reasons are apparent.

1. First, many more members get a better (and early) idea of what your consultation is about.
2. Next, it broadens the base of ownership. In a few instances, the vote also can lessen risk of lawsuit outcomes.

Often at the same voting meeting, the congregation selects the consultation's coordinator. Occasionally, a small committee has been named, rather than a single coordinator.

AUTHORIZATION

In this day and age, and especially in conflicted churches, even bishops and popes do not have the authority we used to think they had. Neither your denomination's endorsements nor your own certifiable skills are enough to authorize the team's credibility for that congregation. If your try to rely on your skills for credibility, quick burn-out is virtually assured. Moreover, you need more than a threshold acceptance level of credibility.

Keep these two points in mind.

1. The host system—not the process, method or consulting personnel—determines authorization and credibility. Therefore, if you are going to work within churches, your *process must harmonize with their distinctive belief system.* Learn all you can from other methods and procedures, from conflict resolution or conflict management, but refrain from relying on their assumptions, concepts or terminology. That would be a case of mixing apples with oranges.
2. Your Sunday morning Bible class presentation will flick the switch which turns on your team's credibility circuits with that congregation. You may have

offered interpretive bursts of bridge-building between behaviors and beliefs during some interviews, but I cannot emphasize enough the importance of the open presentations.

EXPECTATIONS

The less you know about conflict in church systems, the more risk there is that the team will say something dumb, such as: "We recommend that the pastor should leave" (stay, retire). You all but invite lawsuits—a favorite charge is "unlawful deprivation of income," plus a variety of slander rulings. The more you behave like judges, the more likely you are to face one.

Or, are they to expect you to wave some magic wand over them? (I always forget to bring mine.) Rather than coming there as "fixers," you are there as "more help from the church" and as "fellow saints." The third and (possibly) second steps of Matthew 18:15-20 establish their expectations of your team.

RESPONSIBILITY

The more conflict dysfunctional a congregation or pastor, the more care must be taken to provide enough what-to-do's to encourage them without subverting their need to take corporate and personal responsibility. If you leave things too vague, they will keep on floundering. A blurred forest invites regression to focus on just one or two trees. If, on the other hand, you lay out an 83-step "program," it co-opts their initiative.

INTERVIEWS AND GROUP SESSIONS

Several guidelines have become keys to effective use of personal interviews:

1. Interviews that last only 15-20 minutes are a waste of everybody's time. You get trapped in gripes, and you will have heard 99 percent of them by the second interview. I never interview for less than 45 minutes nor more than an hour. That gives you time to track church strengths, personal concerns and needs underlying surface issues, as well as to start building bridges between belief and behaviors.

2. Watch the setting! Never interview in the pastor's office. Setting heavily influences expectations. Move interviews to a motel conference facility or other suitable place if nothing is available at church.

3. Taking notes is perceived as taking evidence. So is anybody's use of a recorder, and that corrupts your role and the process. If you must write something, do it between interviews.

4. Limit the number of relationships in any interview. An individual, couple, two old friends, parent(s) and child(ren): one of these and no more. Otherwise, you will overload/short-circuit the interview, wasting their time and yours.

5. Discourage interviewees' scripts. Those lacking confidence in themselves or the process are prone to come in with some kind of statement. Solid preparations prior to the consultation usually eliminates the problem. If it does not, injecting questions which can engage confidence helps to get the script laid aside.

6. Encourage systemic concerns. "What does this congregation need, over the long term?" helps move interviewee beyond fixation on individuals and presenting issues.

7. Interview one (or a group) of the congregation's back-door losses. Include a usually revealing question:

"What else was happening in your life about the time you left Bethany?"

8. Post a list of those being interviewed on a wall near the room. When somebody sees that other cohorts are coming in, there is less compulsion to dump their whole load on you.

GROUP SESSIONS

Include group sessions to give you a better idea of how individual members associate in *groups* at this church. This may mean council, a board or two, or an open meeting. Without putting too much credence in it, do note body language at these sessions. Yet, steer clear of group dynamics stuff. Because their interaction probably is short-circuited, pull the groups' focus toward you as a step in engaging them with the process.

MOVE ON THREE TRACKS

A *congregation* track discerns systemic short-circuits and detours for sorting things out; no less systemic is your track on what can be done about it.

A *parsonage* track not only picks up on old hurts and isolation amidst trouble, but their future in marriage and family—in symphony with vocation. Your insights and next steps are shared with them collegially, *not* with the congregation. (In some denominations, it can be explained to the congregation constitutionally or traditionally: the District/Diocese/Synod has "supervision" over its clergy. For others, it can be stated as: we find it is most productive to share our insights and recommendations in personal conversation.)

The third track is _relationships,_ with a view to probable Audication as a key follow-up component. What disrupted and distressed relationships here need is our early attention if the congregation's vitality is going to have a chance to get back on track.

REPORT AND FOLLOW UP

It is very important that you present an extensive three-part oral report to the congregation before you leave. Have a member or two use their video cameras to record it. The report should have three parts: What do we have to account for, how can we sort it out, what can you do about it? I always wait three to five weeks before sending a written version of this report. Living with the video version discourages habits of lifting sentences or portions from the report, disregarding the rest.

Follow up is at once an anxiety for congregations and clergy (who feel they have already "gone through this alone too long") and a major reason why only regional jurisdictions should provide access to the process and your team. Before leaving, set agendas and expectations in their minds. Divide up responsibilities within the team.

COSTS

The actual costs for this service should be borne by the congregation, as much as possible. Put bluntly: "freebies" tend to perpetuate congregational dysfunction. A dollar per adult member has been suggested as rule of thumb. We have also noticed how "that is impossible!" changes as the dates near. Individual members start contributing extra dollars as they become better informed about the consultation's possibilities.

Audicators:
Selection, Training and Best Use

More and more denominations, usually under regional auspices and initiatives, are using teams of people
to work on-site with congregations in conflict. Since 50
percent or more of most judicatory leaders' time and
energy are co-opted by troubled parish situations,
Audicators can help those judicatories work more effectively while benefiting congregations.

Two traits are apparent from Audicators' work thus far:

1. drop-outs are virtually unheard of, and
2. Audicator teams are able to work with congregations at any stage, whether for church vitality
   agendas or at conflict dysfunction stages.

One Bishop reports using his Audicators in more
than forty congregations thus far, about a third of his
constituency. One reason is their capability for working
with churches on vitality matters as well as conflict.

SELECTION OF AUDICATORS

Selection of Audicators is made by the District Presi-
dent/Bishop/Superintendent rather than by asking for
volunteers (or being elected). The only class of constitu-
ents who should be excluded from the group are those
who, constitutionally, could be required to be part of an
Adjudication process. Circuit Counselors in the LC-MS,
for example, have been in many of my workshops but
are neither selected nor used as District Audicators, for
that reason.

As a general rule of thumb, the richer the mix of skills
and experience among your Audicators, the better they
work together. Ph.D.'s, homemakers, farmers, pastors,

business executives, regional staff: the range of persons selected for this function is drawn from varied vocational offices.

How many audicators should be chosen? The most useful range has been a number equal to about ten to fifteen percent of your constituent congregations, with several jurisdictions training closer to 20 percent.

With too few audicators, you risk
   a) wearing them out
   b) skimping on follow-up potential for congregations
   c) delay in deploying a team, and
   d) being too limited in the choice of teams best suited to a specific site.

TRAINING FOR AUDICATORS

Two days back-to-back or several weeks apart seem to work best for instruction time, provided it is followed by hands-on experience with the instructor(s) at one or more site consultations. When training, I use an extensive and detailed *Audicators Manual* which consists almost entirely of procedural information.

The longer your time span for training, the more top-flight prospective Audicators you risk excluding. Why? Because they tend to be among your busiest people. They come expecting intensive learning rather than a lot of time-consuming group dynamics.

Hands-on experience aspects of the training process best focuses upon actual on-site consultations with congregations. If your jurisdiction is somewhat localized, one of these consultations can be enough. Even though some Audicators can come only for a few hours of the event, strongly encourage them to do so. Most of the whole group hopefully will be able to devote a day or more.

a) Audicators sit in on interviews as the instructor's *partners,* not as trainees when their presence is to be explained to those being interviewed. I often add: "because we find it helps a church for follow-up work."

b) The 15-minute break between interviews is for explaining, discussing and teaching, as are mealtimes. Audicating partners typically ask questions like: "Why did you do this? Why did you ask that? What were you looking for?"

c) The sooner after their workshop training this hands-on experience can happen, the better. Otherwise, it is too easy for your Audicators to regress back into pre-conceived ideas and attitudes.

USE OF AUDICATORS

Once selected and trained, Audicators are not on their own. It has been that way since the early church. Several suggestions can be drawn from experience.

1. Deployment of Audicators

Typically, a distressed congregation invites regional leadership to meet with them about their difficulties. If it is not an adjudication matter, use of an Audicators team may be helpful. While the surface issues may signal a conflicted congregation, it is important to emphasize that the main reason these Audicators are willing to give their personal time and best efforts to do this is because they find it satisfying to help churches who want to do better. *Wanting to do better:* this emphasis starts to improve the agenda, moving it beyond merely "settling things and quieting things down around here." For other actions necessary at such an informational meeting, refer to our previous outline under "Preparation."

After explaining the jurisdiction's resource of Audicators and what they seek to accomplish, they could vote then and there. Or, a special congregational meeting may be necessary. Date-setting and other arrangements, even selection of a Coordinator, can be referred to Council after authorization action has been taken.

It is important for you to accent Audicators as a *service* of the congregation's regional affiliation. Denominations forget what regional units cannot forget: church and clergy loyalty flows to wherever the most-needed *service* comes from. Loyalty and dollar support never flow to where *programs* originate but rather to the source of *service*.

2. Team

A five-member Audicator team has been normal for most congregations. Division of labor is one reason, given people's other obligations: two on the *parsonage track,* three on the *congregational track.* The more highly polarized the situation, the more care must be exercised in putting together your mix of Audicators.

3. Preparation

We have mentioned the importance of congregational preparation. But how much should the team know about the congregation's situation before it gets there? As little as possible. I find that the only really useful information is what I get face-to-face.

4. Follow-up

Congregations usually remain tentative about Audication teams unless and until they specifically commit to follow-through efforts with that church. This may be

a corollary to the isolating effects of suffering, the loneliness which so often attends troubled times. Prior to its
oral report and consultation closure, a team should
agree on its division of labor for continuing work there.
Decide who will concentrate on the *parsonage* track, who
will focus on the *council and boards* track, and provide
whatever intensive Audication sessions may be indicated.

Above all, the follow-up theme has to be: *Vitality!*
"Most of you want Bethany to do better. We think you
can. Here are some first steps toward making that
happen."

Congregational Follow-Up—"Intensive Audication" for congregational follow-up is a modified version
of the process described under Step Two in our chapter
on Matthew 18. Pairs of conflictors are identified whose
relationship has become so polarized or dysfunctional
as to present an obstacle to the congregation's systemic
renewal.

Where there is conflict between the pastor and several members, have an Audicator[s] meet with the pastor and one member, per time. Expect several two-hour
sessions per pairing. We have found that the first hour
usually gets taken up with an exchange of speeches, the
"I have something to say" sort of thing. Not much
progress happens until the Audicator[s] can interrupt
with "You already said that today."

Council and Boards Follow-Up—Council and
Boards follow-up aspects center on sitting-in and interpretation. A key principle here is to avoid co-opting or
undermining members' initiatives and responsibility.
Encouragement is as valuable as whatever step-by-step
information is requested. I get a lot of these phone calls;

so will you. Sometimes, it helps move things along as much as your time in their meetings might. Timely access to you is important, although there will be times when you wonder why that person called you.

Parsonage Follow-Up—Parsonage follow-up always takes on an agenda clearly distinct from congregation's follow-up. At the outset, Audicators should clarify with the pastor and spouse what will and will not be passed on to the regional office. I usually mention three things I will pass on:

a) my estimate of the pastor's and pastor's spouse's good faith participation,
b) additional help or resources which may be indicated (such as use of a 2-day sorting out session at a ministry-assessment center for both husband and wife), and
c) my opinion on whether, when and how this pastor should seek another call or position.

What else gets passed on? Only what we agree upon! Remind pastors that only two other conditions limit confidentiality: state law and a matter which marks clear violation of ordination vows or policy for your denomination. This second constraint has many centuries of precedent behind it (in canon law, for instance). Though revelation of capital crimes could be kept confidential, the one hearing confession was obligated to inform his bishop (within 24 hours!) of ordination violations—e.g. breaking vows of chastity. Terminated and repentant behavior did not need to be reported. In other words, confidentiality is *not* broken but honored if state law and/or ordination vows mandate appropriate revelation of confidential information.

Sorely conflicted pastors tend to be selective listeners, hearing from you only what they want to hear. In these situations, I find that the pastor's spouse becomes an active ally of the process. So, at key times, you should meet with *both* of them together, as a couple.

At least once a year, have all your Audicators get together to compare notes and experiences, review the past year's sites' situations and look ahead. This effort goes beyond reinforcement and into the important realm of paying their satisfaction wages to your Audicator volunteers.

Afterword

Keep Audicators insulated from your denomination's juridical measures. Audicators' environment is assistance to conflictors' personal/direct solution efforts, Steps One through Three of Matthew 18. Biblically and technically, your Step Four apparatus and procedure are a distinct genre, even while purposes and objectives of the first four Steps should be the same. If you can relate Audicators' roles and Step Four necessities in that *purposeful* context, there is less likelihood of undermining either agenda.

To the best of my knowledge, Audicators trained and functioning over the past several years are all still "on board." That fact contrasts sharply with the huge burnout and drop-out rate in denominational jurisdictions that trained people for "conflict resolution" work with congregations. Why this marked difference? Many reasons have been suggested. Perhaps they get down to this: Audicators' satisfaction wages are a *lot* higher.

15

Usages

▭

These usages could become gimmicky if used in place of informed growth in—and purposeful reliance upon—biblical doctrine. However, they originated as helps to specific people who sincerely wanted to move onto the pathways of Christian forgiveness with each other. "But I do not know how to *begin*," they said.

You may find the three items helpful for your own experience and for others you know. The "Bond of Peace" refers to that mark of the True Church and of all Christian relationships, which the Apostle Paul cites in Ephesians 4:3. In addition to these three items, we have used several others which have more limited use: a "Peace Agreement Service" for use after successful Intensive Audication, a brief "Consultation Bond of Peace Service" which concludes an on-site consultation, and a "Collegial Bond of Peace Service" for use at a denomination's/region's pastoral conferences.

Please feel free to adapt services in this Chapter for use. For the samples given here, some introductory comments are in order.

Congregational Bond of Peace

This originated as an early follow-up event, usually about three months after an on-site consultation. A number of congregations also have been using their own versions of it annually at New Years. This is an occasion to let go of the previous year's hurts as members move into a new year.

Note on rubrics: during a vacancy, some congregations have used the oral naming-of-the matter option. However, most have found use of the "Dear Lord Letter" less intimidating to members. If the Letter is used, provision for the letters' immediate ritual destruction must be arranged. Usually they are all burned toward the service's conclusion. One congregation burned them in a round charcoal broiler in front of the altar and set off all the smoke alarms! Proceed with whatever receptacle you use to a place where the Letters can be burned without risk of asphyxiation.

THE SERVICE

The occasion for this Congregational service is to experience how God's Word enables us to really *forget*—let go of—the pain and power of old hurts, angers, and sins which break the Bond of Peace which should mark Christ's church among us. Why? So that we can delight and grow once more in the One New Person relationships God has created for us, and to get on with our mutual ministry. So long as the Past runs amok in our lives—not only in my conscience but in marriage and family, in vocation and neighboring, and here within our congregation—we're handing Satan a loaded gun to use against us. The Service applies ancient biblical custom and authority to our problems with the Past so that it can become the green pasture of assurance rather than the killing field of old guilts and hurts.

Preparation is essential for the Service's effectiveness. Otherwise, the occasion may become little more than going through the motions, may become a careless "magic wand" or excuse to avoid facing up to what's really gone wrong among us. Personal and group Bible study, preaching, teaching and discussion should prepare the way for this Service. (Sample Scriptural references are listed below.) In years to come, the congregation may renew benefits from the Service, using it on occasions such as New Year's time, during Lent, prior to a Pastor's departure or arrival, at the conclusion of a major congregational project or building program. Past hurts must be dealt with! A Bond of Peace service provides and points to the foundation for facing—and then letting go of—that Past.

FOR YOUR PREPARATION:

God's Peace Blessing	*Forgive and Forget*
Psalm 133	Psalm 25:7; 51:1, 9
Ephesians 2:13-22	Isaiah 43:25
Ephesians 4:1-6	Matthew 18:18; John 20:23
I Corinthians 6:1-8	Mark 11:23-25
Galatians 6:1-5	Hebrews 8:12; 10:17
James 3:13-18	Leviticus 16:15-22; 34

Our Ministry
Matthew 18:12-35
Romans 14:7-20
II Corinthians 5:17-21
Ephesians 4:15-16
Colossians 3:12-15

Greeting (*Congregation, please remain seated*)
Beloved in Christ, God knows all about you but loves you nonetheless!
The grace of our Lord Jesus Christ, the love of God, and the communion of the Holy Spirit be with you all.
AND ALSO WITH YOU.

Occasion
(*A designated member stands with the Presider before the people*)

(*Presider*) Almighty God, we are the people of your Son, Jesus Christ, Prince of Peace. You have commanded us to be Peace-builders in his name. You have provided us with all we need to fulfill this command.
OUR HELP IS IN THE NAME OF THE LORD.

(*Designated member*) Therefore, we come now to name in our hearts and in your presence those hurtful matters which attack the Bond of Peace in Christ you created among us, to name them in order to let go of them at last. By our personal actions and inactions that Deceiver, that Prince of Lies, that Anti-Christ Accuser and our Old Foe, Satan, has worked to cripple or even kill the One New Persons you created for our life together and for our delight.

We have come so many times before to claim your entire forgiveness of our sin. But now we come for your entire *forgetting* of our sins, to remember them no more, for your binding their killing power to the moment of your forgiveness, as you did for your People through Aaron on the Day of Atonement, and as Christ empowered the apostles—and us— to do.

Almighty God, renew each and all of us in Christ that we may delight and grow again in our One New Person relationships. But also that our mutual ministry might surge and pulse with new life, so that souls will be saved, the wounded healed, your beloved world rejoice in the harvest of our faithfulness in readiness for your return. O Lord, restore now your Alpha-and-Omega power among us. Our times—our Past and Future—are in your hands!
COME, LORD JESUS! ALPHA-AND-OMEGA,
REMEMBER MY SIN NO MORE!

Hymn: "Love Divine, All Loves Excelling"

Invocation (Congregation, please stand)
In the name of the Father and of the ✢ Son and of the Holy Spirit.
AMEN.

Beloved in Christ, we have been gathered here by God in his remembrance of our baptism into Christ to be Peace-Builders in His name, as He commanded us, and to celebrate His Bond of Peace in the Lord's Supper. Let us pray.

Lord Jesus Christ, Prince of Peace, you are gracious and merciful, slow to anger, abundant in compassionate love. Be present among us now to forgive and forget the matters we name which cause trouble and heartache in our life. Some among us hurt so much and others present anguish with them. All of us, the whole Body of Christ, suffer when one of us is troubled. But then, you told us that this would and should be so.

- Remember your Body here so that we can reach out in compassion toward each other as toward you, to see your face in our times with one another.

- Remember your One New Person creations here so that we can forgive and forget in your name and for the sake of those relationships, even while our natural feelings may still be bloated with pride and self-righteousness.

- Remember all you have accomplished and are doing even now among us. Open our eyes to these things so we can know God's Peace in our hearts at last.
AMEN.

Scripture (*Congregation, please be seated.*)

Hear the Word of the Lord, from the third chapter of St. Paul's letter to the Colossians: *Therefore, as God's chosen people, holy and dearly beloved, clothe yourselves with compassion, kindness, humility, gentleness and patience. Bear each other's burdens and forgive whatever grievance as you may have against one another. And over all these virtues put on love, which binds them all together in perfect symphony. Let the Peace of Christ rule in your hearts, since as members of one body your were called to his Peace.* This is the Word of the Lord.
THANKS BE TO GOD.

Hymn: "O God of Mercy, God of Light"

Scripture (*Congregation, please stand*)

Hear the Gospel of the Lord, according to St. Matthew, the fifth chapter: *But I say to you that everyone who is anger with his neighbor shall be liable to judgment; whoever insults his neighbor shall be liable to the church. And whoever says 'You Fool' will be in danger of the fires of hell.*

Therefore, if you are offering your gift at the altar and there remember that your neighbor has something against you, leave your gift there in front of the altar. First go and be reconciled to your neighbor; then come and offer your gift. This is the Gospel of our Lord.
PRAISE TO YOU, O CHRIST.

Homily
(Congregation, please be seated.)

Meditation: a time for considering your specific opportunities and initiatives for Peace-building—in your personal relationships and/or in a troubled relationship with another person in the congregation. (It may be helpful to describe—or review and revise—the situation on your "Dear Lord" letter.)

Invitation *(Congregation, please stand)*

Beloved in Christ, we stand in God's presence in obedience to the command of Christ that we be Peace-builders with each other and enter into the eternal blessing which God has promised to all who build Peace in His name with others. Now it is time and necessary to name those matters which injure or break the Bond of Peace among us, those things also which have been a poison in the Body of Christ, so that we can let go of them as our Alpha-Omega Lord for us remembers these things no more.

Therefore, in Christ's name, I invite you to bring your Letters forward in the same custom we use for processing to the Lords Supper.

(Participants come to the Altar rail, surrender their Letters in turn, and kneel. The Presider will ask each of you:)

Do you desire that the matters you have named be forgiven by Christ? If so, then say your Amen.
AMEN.

Receive from Christ himself the entire forgiveness and forgetting of each and all those things you have confessed which break His Bond of Peace in your life. In the name of the Father and of the Son and of the Holy Spirit. Amen.

(The Presider then seals each person with the sign of the Cross:)
Live now in our Lord's Bond of Peace!

(When all have returned to their seats: Congregation, please stand.)
Let us pray. Blessed are you, O Lord, Creator of the universe and Prince of Peace. You have promised to bless for all eternity our ministry of reconciliation with each other in your Bond of Peace. Therefore, in obedience to the command of Jesus Christ and by his authority, I declare this to you: the sins they have

confessed have already been forgiven by you, O Lord, and bound to this moment! Their Peace-Breaking shall have no more power over them or among them from this time forth! Amen. *(The Presider then faces the congregation.)*

Dear Christians:

Know also that if, on your own private authority, you release the power of sin which God himself has forgiven and forgotten, God will return this iniquity upon your life and for your eternal condemnation.

Stand firm, therefore, in Christ! He has freed you from your sin's murderous power. Our heavenly Father has been waiting for you and welcomes you back home!

Let us rejoice in this enormous Blessing of God with the 133rd Psalm (in unison):
BEHOLD, HOW BLESSED IT IS FOR ALL TO LIVE TO-GETHER IN SYMPHONY: IT IS LIKE PRECIOUS OIL UPON YOUR FOREHEAD FLOWING DOWN YOUR FACE AS IT DID DOWN AARON'S FACE TO THE COLLAR OF HIS CLOTHES; ABUNDANT AS THE DEW ON MOUNT HER-MON FALLING ON THE HEIGHTS OF ZION WHERE GOD GIVES HIS BLESSING: EVERLASTING LIFE!

Almighty God, so bless your Bond of Peace among us and through us now and forevermore. Amen!

As is the ancient custom of God's People and as commanded us by our Lord Jesus, before we are gathered together again for the Lord's Supper, I invite you to seek out each other in this assembly and to claim God's Bond of Peace among you. Do so now, not on your own authority, but with this declaration: "God's Peace is ours!"

(When personal initiatives have concluded, the congregation may be seated.)

The Lord's Supper
Let us pray together our Lord's Prayer.
(We pray, in unison.)

Let us confess our faith together with the Apostles' Creed.
(We confess our faith, in unison.)

Blessed are we whose sins are forgiven and their power forgotten by God. The Lord Jesus Christ has made us free to come now in his Bond of Peace to union with him in the Lord's Supper.

(Congregation, please stand for the Words of Institution. We come forward, according to our usual custom.)

Closing Prayer *(Congregation may remain seated.)*

Let us pray.

We give thanks to you, Almighty God, that you have refreshed us through this salutary gift. And we implore you that of your mercy you would strengthen us through the same in faith toward you and in compassion toward one another; through Jesus Christ, your son, our Lord, who lives and reigns with you and the Holy Spirit, one God, now and forever. AMEN!

Benediction *(Congregation, please stand.)*

The Lord bless you and keep you. The Lord make his face shine upon you and be gracious to you. The Lord look upon you with favor and ✛ give you peace.

Hymn: "Blest Be the Tie that Binds"

Offering of Dear Lord Letters

(The congregation moves/processes to the place where these letters shall be burned, in the redeeming presence of Jesus Christ in his Body.)

GO FORTH IN THE PEACE OF CHRIST!

O, Christian: You think that thing is too awful for Christ's love to heal? Are you worse than the world around you? You read the papers, watch TV news. You are worse than *that*? But isn't this the "world" God so loved that he sent his only Son to restore it unto himself, even so? Are you any worse than what's going on— anywhere—these days? God loves the world and He loves you, *too*! So, why are you doubting God loves the likes of you? This service is for *you*: so you can finally "name" that Thing and let go of it, into the loving arms of Jesus!

The Dear Lord Letter

The "Dear Lord Letter" is simple. Completed, it is sealed in an envelope for use at this service. Of course, a member may present more than one Letter.

Dear Lord, the matter is this:

This is what it has done to our relationships:

This is what needs to happen, for that relationship's vitality:

Individual Bond of Peace

"My brother is dead. He stole my inheritance. How can I forgive my brother, as Christ requires, when he is not here?" Or, perhaps your pain centers on someone from your childhood who is dead or in locations unknown, or someone who under no circumstances is willing to take part in healing efforts with you.

It might be helpful to bring a fellow saint for this occasion. Participants have found this especially useful for a forgiveness dialogue. "Martha took my ex-husband's part several times when I came back to the pew," this Christian told me. "She did not defend or excuse him but she prodded me into seeing things I had not named and yet needed to let go of in God's presence."

THE SERVICE

This "Forgiveness" usage is intended for occasions when one or more other parties to Peace-breaking cannot or will not participate (for example, deceased parents). Recourse to this usage is appropriate after your prayerful and good faith work with the "Forgiveness Pathways" outline and Matthew 18 suggestions from *Peace in the Parish*, and only when no possibility for timely participation by the other person(s) exists. You may have further opportunities for use of this personal service, perhaps as more of Satan's deceptions are pulled aside concerning this particular relationship or for other situations. Be reminded, though, that your Bond of Peace lives in *relationships* and may be subverted if you use this service as a means to avoid faithful One New Person reconciliation with the other person(s). The day may yet come when this service may be a mutual experience for you with that one.

Setting

Preferred: Come to your church sanctuary so that you may go to the altar when ready. (Either consult with the pastor or secretary beforehand for a quiet time in the sanctuary, "for a time of personal prayer and meditation.") It can be helpful to have a trusted fellow saint accompany you.

Alternative: Your favorite personal setting for prayer and devotional study or meditation.

Process

1. *Preparation:* Before coming to the altar, while seated or kneeling, meditate upon God's Name—*Alpha and Omega*—and on His work of *Remembrance.*

a. Do this "historically" as well as "personally." Recall those instances which come to mind from Scripture and throughout the history of God's care for His People, instances which have meaning to you about the matter that brings you here. Not "concepts" but specific instances in which God dealt with Abraham or Sarah, Paul, Mary, Rachel in a redemptive way, instances which resemble your situation. *This is essential for any prayer petition which would be in His Name!* For example, in spoken prayer: "O Lord, remember how you interceded and cared for _____ when _____? And how you redeemed _____ in his/her time of trouble with _____? (If you can recall further instances, do so. Then:) Now for (this situation/need) in my life, would you deal with me (us) in these same ways once more?" Take time. Repeat this spoken prayer as further instances occur to you.

b. Do this in certain confidence that God *remembers* (makes it effective in the present) His redeeming acts for "thousands of generations." And that means *you,* too! Therefore, the purpose of your meditation on God's Name is to submit your Service's petition to the redeeming certainty of God's Alpha-and-Omega *remembrance.*

c. Meditate also on the "Omega" (His lordship over the present-participating *future)* of His Name...for your situation: not only for your anxieties but also for your decisive priorities, for release from suffocating captivity to this Present (and Past) thing, so that you may be able to "dance with delight even in the things unsettled." Here, again, use spoken prayer to remember biblical/historic instances: "O Lord, remember how your promises worked in (David's life when he was so burdened down with [Absalom, his enemies]? And also with the Psalmist, when he was so beset by the Accuser over the memory of his sins as a younger man? And with _____, whose confident Hope in your Lordship over (his/her) years to come redeemed (him/her) in that affliction with _____? O Lord, Alpha-and-Omega Lord, would you deal with me now in these same ways?") Take time. Repeat this spoken prayer as further examples occur to you.

2. *Naming:* Come to the altar (or tabernacle), facing it at or between the rail if your church has one. In ancient times, you would at least begin this portion of the Service *standing.* (Kneel throughout, if you prefer. And, unless doing so is a barrier to you, continue with your eyes open, addressing the altar and cross.) *"O Lord, my Lord, the matter is this."* (Describe the situation you are bringing to Christ.)

a. *Striving:* (This ancient biblical practice may be appropriate amidst confusion over God's apparent—to you—departure from His Alpha-Omega ways. You should return to the pew after *each* Striving to search your heart for God's redemptive remembering, e.g. for soul-searching over "*to what end* has He dealt with me this way?" Do *not* focus this search on "punishment!" Not if you are Striving *in His Name.*)

1) "Lord God, my God, why have you dealt with me in these ways?" (Be specific, not only about what has happened but also its effect on your One New Person relationships.)

2) "*Remember* me, O Lord, remember my life as you did _____, in (his/her) trouble like mine."

(Pause. Meditate on this question: are there any *differences* from you in how your cited Predecessor discerned and acted?)

3) "O Lord, God of _____ (that Predecessor) and my God, hide not thy face from me in this matter. Show me what you are accomplishing—and would do—through my life." (Do not expect or demand quick and complete insight; Satan— that Deceiver—is too crafty in his devices which blind us to what God is doing in our life.) If the Service does *not* include the **Striving** portion, preface the next step with: "*Nonetheless, I have....*"

b. *Announcing:* "*I have named and confessed this matter to you, O Lord, in order to let go of it, to be released from its power over me, so that I may grow and delight in the peace you created for me.*"

3. *Release* of the other person(s): when and if he / she / they cannot (or, won't) participate with you.

a. "*Lord Jesus, This matter has done* _____ *(specify) to the US which you created and to which you bonded* _____*(specify) and me.*"

b. "*We have sinned against your wondrous creation for us, O Lord, in breaking your Bond of Peace.*" (If such is the case, add: "*and in the death of that One New Person you created for us.*")

c. "*Now before your altar, I release* (name) _____ *from my remembrance of this matter, and commend* (him / her / them) *to your Remembrance. This release from all Peace-breaking power over my life in Thee I claim solely by your Almighty and eternal Alpha-and-Omega Name,*" (Make the sign of the Cross.) "*Father, Son, Holy Spirit. Amen!*"

(You should know, then, that while you may "recall" him / her / them and the matter, all "remembrance" [*power to kill/break* your *other* One New Person relationships] has been "cast into the depths of the sea" by our Almighty Lord of Time! And...the "No Fishing" sign is up for you, from now on!)

4. *Forget in Forgiveness:* Now, you can claim the biblical authority to Forget in Forgiveness, given to His People in Leviticus 16, renewed and empowered for all those who are in Christ. (For this portion, you may prefer to kneel.)

a. "*Heavenly Father, in the name of Christ, I claim your forgiveness for my own sin in this matter, for my neglect and also for my willful submission to Satan's deceptions.*" (Name—specifically—*each* of your God's Peace-Breaking behaviors *and* attitudes relating to this matter, as well as the other person / people.)

b. *"Heavenly Father, in the name of Christ and for the sake of the One New Person life you created for me with others no less than with You, O Lord, I forgive* (name) *as you have forgiven me. As I now forgive* (name), *you already will have forgiven* (him/her/them) *for this sin against you and against the relationship you gave us. Thank you, Father: Bless now this Forgiveness, in Jesus name."* (Pause, in confidence that God has accomplished this with your Intercession.)

c. *"Heavenly Father, in the name of Christ, I Forget this sin. This hurtful sin which you have Forgiven shall have no more power or life in any relationship you have given me. It has been cast away as far as east · is from the west, its entire power bound by you to this moment of Forgiveness. Thank you, Almighty God: Bless this Forgetting forever more, in Jesus name. Amen!*

5. *Building* upon God's action of Forgetting in Forgiveness: return to your seat and consider your definite next steps for *building* upon God's gift of his peace to your life. Before concluding this service, be sure to consider and evaluate the following:

a. *Discernment*—right now, what new insights into (for example) what *really* happened are beginning to emerge? (When we have seen "light at the end of the tunnel" during a redemptive occasion such as this, we often begin to see more clearly those things which were too indistinct—or frightening—before healing became certain.)

b. *Changes*—make three decisions about changes/new emphases in your life which build upon what God has accomplished with you in this service. Focus them on one (or more) of your One New Person relationships rather than on your "private" existence.

c. *Conclusion*—return to your place before the altar and, audibly, speak to your Lord:
Lord Jesus, thank you for the blessing of Forgiveness you have now given to me and through me to (name). *I have decided to build upon this blessing in these ways: 1)* _____ *2)* _____, *3)* _____. *Grant me not only the power to accomplish these but also grant me an open heart and mind to discern new opportunities for Peace-Building in my life. In the Name of the Father, Son, and Holy Spirit. Amen.*

Forgiveness Pathways

To add more breadth to this experience, it should be helpful to refer to our explanatory suggestions for use of Matthew 18's first two steps. Take special care for the *setting* in which you use this sequence, a setting which implies any kind of *turf* can torpedo this usage. If your church sanctuary is selected, take care lest your physical positioning and manner connote implied superiority or inferiority. (Pastors!) As with the Individual service, consider the wisdom and worth of having a fellow saint sit in with both/all of you.

How does Forgiveness *work* among Christians? We want to get on with it but are uncertain about the "how to" steps to take and what to say. Most of Matthew 18 focuses on how Forgiveness works. Specifically, these "Pathways" suggestions may be helpful in your personal response to God's Word in verse 15 of that chapter. In Step One (in the verses 15-20) pathways to Forgiveness and reconciliation, you take the initiative and *go* to the other person(s)—regardless of who "started it" or who is "wrong." Keep in mind that this passage provides back-up further Steps (e.g. working with a "fellow saint" Audicator, verse 16) in the event you are not successful...the first time. As with any resource for God's Peace-building, this strategy canstand only upon a Christ-centered foundation. Guided by prayer and Bible study, your efforts are sustained and insights are inspired in the Holy Spirit.

A. INVENTORY *your US relationships.*

1. What are your US relationships? Name/list each one and the specific people with whom you have been bonded by God in a One New Person. Remember: in some of the biblical US categories (e.g. Vocation, Church, Family, Neighbor) you may be bonded in *several* of these relationships.

2. Write down a list of the *hurts* in each of these relationships, not only your hurts or those wounds between the two (or more) of you, but also in the other person's life. Are there hurts for him/her which haven't been named or healed? Not gripes or

complaints, but *hurts*: those action/reaction wounds which threaten (or have already broken) the Peace-bonding between you.

B. STRATEGIZE each list.

1. What *really* happened? Remember that the longer it has been, the more likely that other problems have been "deflected" onto this one.

2. What e*lse* was happening in your life—the other "hassles"— when trouble hit this US? By the same token, can you recall whether the other person(s) were going through similar distractions at that time?

3. What has all this done to the *other* person(s)? You have already spent far too much time on what its done to *you*.

4. What has this matter been doing to your *other* US relationships? Again, not to *you*, privately, but what has it done to *those* other US's?

5. What has it done to *this* US--not to your own ME/private feelings. Has the way you (you both) have handled this trouble collapsed your US down to—at best—a WE, for example? (US is in the objective case—it *receives* your actions; WE is a much inferior ego relationship.)

6. What's got to happen for the sake of this—and of your other— US's? Not to "settle" all the issues: what has got to happen for the US relationship so tha*t* both of you can live graciously in God's Peace with each other...despite still-unsettled issues?

C. INITIATE Peace-Building. Remember Peter's question and Christ's response in Matthew 18:21-22, because taking the initiative only "just this once" is not *good faith.*

1. If the other person(s) are deceased or, in truth, not accessible, consider adapting the *Individual Bond of Peace Service* to your Forgiveness Pathways.

2. Formulate several Approach scenarios for your initiative. The longer the Bond of Peace has been broken and the more entrenched the feelings, the more likely it is that brick walls have risen between you. Taking the initiative does not mean banging your head against those walls. It usually means varied approaches which help *both* of you go *around* (or over) those walls.

3. Emphasize that the matter is something which you (both of you?) need to *let go of.* Even if the US has died. Even if the "issues" will not, or cannot, be settled. And, "we are not going to get bogged down on who's Right or Wrong."

D. *AGENDA for Peace-Building Session.* This Agenda amounts to the direct application of your Inventory and Examination preparations.

1. "_____, remember when _____? What *really* happened back then?" (Time confuses our memories; it does mine.)

2. "When somebody is hurt, it is too easy to get wrapped up with what it has done to **me.** But, _____, was *something else* going on in each of our lives when this thing happened between us?" (Listen, also, for clues whether something from the *Past* was triggered by that episode.)

3. "_____, what has all this been doing to you?" (Listen for and share in the redemptive/growth effects, not just the negatives.)

4. "How has this thing affected each of us in our *other* relationships?" (Parenting and marriage, vocation, church life, Christian life [prayer? Bible study? worship?], friendships/ neighboring? It often helps to look at these "spill-over" impacts, together.)

5. "What we have (had?) is (was?) really greater than both of us put together. What has *how* we have dealt with this thing between us affected our US and our other relationships?"

(Of course, realize that this US may be dead and gone. You are not trying to exhume the body but deal with the disease which killed it, lest that disease infect your— and his or her— other US relationships!)

6. "What has to happen for the sake of *all* our (US) relationships, _____?" (If the trouble or hurt centered in your marriage US, what has to happen for your parenting/family US, your vocation and church relationships, etc.? E.g. don't confine healing just to the marriage.)

E. *SOLUTION planning.* Here is the phase of: Who does What, When, How? Be careful not to drown each other (or your US's) in a deluge of Solution strategies. Conflict Redemption is life-long, day-by-day…not a one-shot try. So, it is a matter of "let's work on these things for starters, those things later, and make revisions as we go."

1. *The Past:* Specify other troubles or hurts from our Past which we can work at *naming* and *letting go* of…for the sake of the Future as well as the Present (All of us should be aware in this day and age of the fact that beneath a Past hurt-episode often lies another Past hurt that wasn't dealt with or let go of.)

2. *Deceptions:* This aspect of your work depends on application of biblical insights on the doctrine of Righteousness. We get "snookered" by *Satan's* wily deceptions, by this Deceiver. We get blinded by these often trivial/little things to what God has already created among us, already given to us. By taking the Deceiver seriously, we can avoid the dead ends of fault-finding, of guilty-innocent party branding and similar unChristian gimmicks.

3. *Purpose-System:* Remember that conflict dysfunction usu-ally is preceded by collapse of your Purpose System. That collapse isn't a *sudden* thing. Rather, it often happens gradu-ally— like the way credit card debts can mount up— bit by bit into a monster.

a) How have your Purposes been working in *ten* (cite them!) "money" decisions you have made (together?) in the past few months or years? Have lower priorities gotten inflated by how you have spent your money, and on what that purchase or expense signifies to you? What specific steps can you begin to take to restore your Purpose System in money matters?

b) Have you let one US tyrannize the others, cripple your "symphony" of US's? For example, has parenting drowned out your Marriage Melody? Specify the steps both or all of you will take to get these US's back in "symphony."

c) Have you let your Ego/Personal Preference wishes get inflated at expense to your US's? Is your Wish List for "self-fulfillment" chock full of fantasies and self-delusions? (Be honest!) Or, have each/both of you so *submerged* your self-care that it is drowning in the deluge of your Vocation needs? Is *your* side of that US "quarter" getting *blank?* How can you help each other restore *each* side of that coin to "mint condition"...without de-valuing it to two separate "dimes?"

4. *Forgiveness and Forgetting:* Each time you (both?) work through this basic Forgiveness Pathways sequence, it is virtually certain that your prior agendas will be transformed. Not only about what is *really* the trouble but about what has to happen. What needs to be *Forgotten in Forgiveness*...for the sake of claiming God's power of new life in your US?

5. *Bond of Peace:* In such important matters, verbal and intellectual/rational agreements come unstuck too easily, have too little force. When you have (a) named the matter which must be let go, and (b) specified your Peace Agreement (agree in principle on the who-what-how next steps), then bring closure to your Pathways by (c) use of a ritual for the Bond of Peace (Ephesians 4:1-3).

Adapt these three usages to your own situation. But agree on any changes prior to the occasion, with other participants' knowledge and agreement. Bear in mind that these were created for a Lutheran sanctuary setting. Some important adaptations to your own denominational traditions and sensitivities may be in order. Nonetheless, the heart and core of these usages will be appropriate among Christians for whom God's Word has healing authority.

Afterword to Peace in the Parish

My outlook in writing this book was to describe what I saw during the Peace in the Parish project, more than to theorize and construct concepts. That has been a jarring experience for the academician side of my brain but has also changed the pastoral side. It helped a lot to forsake notions of coming up with a Guru-on-the-Subject book and, instead, to keep telling myself: "Jim, you are a child, after all!" Of God, of his Church, of my family's heritage.

Carry my book lightly because none of it is carved in stone. Now it is out of my hands and into yours. May God bless and inspire you in however you use *Peace in the Parish*!

About the Author

James Qualben earned his Ph.D. at Northwestern University (medieval history), an M.A. at the University of Chicago, his M. Div. from Luther-Northwestern Theological Seminary, and his B. A. at Wagner College. A former seminary professor (historical theology, at Wartburg Seminary) and history professor (Carnegie-Mellon University), he has also served eleven years in parish ministry (three congregations in Illinois and Pennsylvania).

The experiential base for this book began with his work in multi-party conflict relating to energy development, among groups in Washington, D.C. and on the Great Plains. That base became parish-focused in his work as National Consultant to the Lutheran Church-Missouri Synod for more than four years. A Lutheran pastor, his "merger geneology" began in the Norwegian Lutheran Church in America, which become the Evangelical Lutheran Church, which joined in the American Lutheran Church, and now is part of the Evangelical Lutheran Church in America. (Can any non-Lutheran follow this?)

James and Lois, his wife of 35 years, live and work together in San Antonio. Their three children-- Susan, Steven, and Michael—also live in Texas. Susan and her obstetrician husband and their daughter, Rachel, live in Austin; Steven is a parish pastor in Victoria; Michael is completing his molecular biology and chemistry majors at Texas Lutheran College. Lois is a native of Minnesota; Jim was born and raised in New York City.

Index

To Order Copies

Telephone Orders: Call 512:822-2521 or 822-4273

Postal Orders: LangMarc Publishing, P. O. Box 33817, San Antonio, Texas 78265-3817. USA.

Please send the following books. I understand that I may return any books for a full refund—for any reason.

PEACE IN THE PARISH: $15.95 soft cover

Number of soft cover copies _____ x $15.95 = $

SHIPPING: **Unless requested otherwise, sent UPS.**
UPS: $2.50 for first book and 75 cents for each additional book. (Delivery usually 5 week days)
Air Mail: $3.50 per book
Book Rate: $2.00 for the first book and 75 cents for each additional book (Postal Service three to four weeks)

Please send payment with order:

BOOKS COST:

SHIPPING:

CHECK ENCLOSED:

NAME and UPS ADDRESS for order delivery:

_____

_____

_____

_____